SINGAPORE
PERSPECTIVES 2016
We

SINGAPORE
PERSPECTIVES 2016
We

Edited by

Teng Siao See
Justin Lee

Institute of Policy Studies, Singapore

Lee Kuan Yew
School of Public Policy
National University of Singapore

iPS Institute of
Policy Studies

World Scientific

Published by

World Scientific Publishing Co. Pte. Ltd.

5 Toh Tuck Link, Singapore 596224

USA office: 27 Warren Street, Suite 401-402, Hackensack, NJ 07601

UK office: 57 Shelton Street, Covent Garden, London WC2H 9HE

British Library Cataloguing-in-Publication Data
A catalogue record for this book is available from the British Library.

SINGAPORE PERSPECTIVES 2016
We

ISBN 978-981-3208-37-7 (pbk)

Desk Editor: Sandhya Venkatesh

Contents

Preface vii
Janadas Devan

Acknowledgements xv

Introduction 1
Justin Lee and Teng Siao See

Panel 1 Collaborative Governance? 5
Speech by Minister Chan Chun Sing
Panel Discussion with Kok Heng Leun, Lee Huay Leng and Eugene Tan

Panel 2 Cohesive Diversity? 35
Speech by Minister Ng Chee Meng
Panel Discussion with David Chan, Elaine Ho and Hassan Ahmad

Panel 3 Inclusive Growth? 63
Speech by Minister Ong Ye Kung
*Panel Discussion with Yeoh Lam Keong, Tan Kong Yam and
Chua Hak Bin*

Panel 4 The Future of "We" 89
Speech by Minister Heng Swee Keat
*Panel Discussion with Ho Kwon Ping, Bilahari Kausikan and
Chan Heng Chee*

Post-conference Reflections

Eugene Tan   125

Elaine Ho   131

Hassan Ahmad   135

Yeoh Lam Keong   139

Chua Hak Bin   143

About the Contributors   **149**

Preface

JANADAS DEVAN

"We" — it is the first word in the Preamble to the Constitution of the United States: "We the People..."

It is also the first word in our National Pledge: "We, the citizens of Singapore..."

It is an example of what in modern rhetorical theory has come to be known as a "catachresis" — a linguistic imposition that brings into existence that which it posits. The "we" in "we the people" is the application of a pronoun "used by a speaker to refer to himself or herself and one or more other people considered together", as the Oxford English Dictionary defines "we", to a much larger grouping of people largely unacquainted with one another — in the US, China or Singapore — thus bringing into existence the "imagined community" that we collectively posit by referring to ourselves as "we".

When it was applied by the framers of the United States Constitution to the "people" of the 13 colonies, they in effect claimed for the people the sovereignty that had hitherto reposed in the king — with the royal "we" thus replaced by the popular "we".

The first time we heard "we" used to describe us was in the famous press conference that the founding prime minister Lee Kuan Yew gave on the occasion of Singapore's separation from Malaysia. We all remember the tears he shed that day when he said he would always look back on our leaving Malaysia as "a moment of anguish".

What most of us forget — till we were reminded of it at the 2015 National Day Parade — was that he had ended the press conference on an altogether different note, with these stirring words: "We are going to have a multiracial nation in Singapore. We will set the example. This is not a Malay nation; this is not a Chinese nation; this is not an Indian nation. Everybody will have his place, equal; language, culture, religion.... And finally, let us, really Singaporeans — I cannot call myself a Malaysian now — we unite, regardless of race, language, religion, culture."

"I cannot call myself a Malaysian now" — that transition from one "imagined community", Malaysian, to another, Singaporean, was fraught with tension.

It is too embarrassing 50 years later to recall the pathos of "I cannot call myself a Malaysian now". We cannot understand why that transition from Malaysian to Singaporean should have been difficult.

Let me further illustrate this with another example, this time a statement made on March 17, 1966, barely seven months after Separation: "A national identity for Singapore is not possible and the very idea itself is ludicrous."

Who said that? Lee Siew Choh? Lim Chin Siong? Possible, since the *Barisan Sosialis* and the Communist Party of Malaya thought Singapore's independence was "phoney". But it was neither Dr Lee Siew Choh nor Mr Lim who uttered this statement.

Perhaps David Marshall then. After all, Mr Marshall authored a number of colourful statements in the course of his career. But alas, this wasn't one among them.

The person who delivered this categorical judgment on the impossibility — the sheer ludicrousness — of a Singaporean "national identity" was none other than S. Rajaratnam, the author of the Singapore National Pledge and the muse of a Singaporean Singapore.

The Straits Times used a stark headline in reporting Mr Rajaratnam's remarks: "Can Singapore Have a Separate National Identity? 'Ludicrous' — Rajaratnam".

The tension I spoke of earlier in referring to Mr Lee's press conference — "I can't call myself a Malaysian now" — can be seen again in the way *The Straits Times* reported the story. Notice how it took care to say "separate national identity". The word "separate" should have been unnecessary. After all, by definition, national identities are separate. So there is no need to insist: "Singapore cannot have a separate national identity". Separate from what?

The clue is provided in what else Mr Rajaratnam said on March 17, 1966: Reunification with Malaysia was "inevitable", he said. The forces of history will bring Singapore and Malaysia together again, he prophesied.

So you see, the subconscious of *The Straits Times* then — for it was still a paper serving both Malaysia and Singapore simultaneously — its subconscious probably still held that Singapore could not have a "separate" national identity apart from Malaysia. Separation was still assumed to be temporary. Singapore may be a separate political entity, for a while, at any rate; but it could not have a separate "national identity".

That Mr Rajaratnam too could hold this view in March 1966 is all the more remarkable when one recalls that he had penned the first draft of the National Pledge just the month before, on February 18. His name has become inseparably linked to the Pledge, but there is also one other name whom we should remember in connection with the Pledge.

RAJARATNAM'S FIRST DRAFT

The idea for the Pledge in fact originated with Mr Ong Pang Boon, then Education Minister. It was he who first proposed that schoolchildren should have a flag-raising ceremony every day, accompanied by the recitation of a Pledge. And it was he who sought Mr Rajaratnam's advice on the wording of the Pledge.

The draft Mr Rajaratnam first produced read thus: "We, *as citizens of Singapore*, pledge ourselves to *forget* differences of race, language and religion and become one united people; to build a democratic society where justice and equality will prevail and where we will seek happiness and progress by helping one another." (The emphases added are mine.)

Note first the weak "we, as citizens of Singapore" — as though there is a distinction between "we" and "citizens of Singapore"; as though the "we" here exceeded, went beyond, mere "citizens of Singapore". Might we hear in this subtle hiatus or gap between "we" and "citizens" the conviction that Mr Rajaratnam expressed a month later — that there can be no such thing as a "Singaporean national identity"?

His implicit, perhaps unconscious, logic seemed to be that Singapore might be a separate political entity — with "citizens" to call its own — but its possession of a national identity awaited fulfilment in the not-so-distant future when we are reunited with Malaysia.

We do not have Mr Rajaratnam's re-drafts or Mr Lee Kuan Yew's edits, but the final version that schoolchildren my age first recited on August 24, 1966, six months later — I remember that day clearly, as though it were yesterday; I was in Primary 6 — began definitively and powerfully thus: "We, the citizens of Singapore".

No hiatus or gap between "we" and "citizens". The "we" that we learnt to call ourselves from that day coincided with "citizens of Singapore". We, thus, came into existence as a collective pronoun: "We".

ACCEPT, NOT FORGET, OUR DIFFERENCES AND THEN GO BEYOND THEM

I draw your attention next to what Mr Rajaratnam's first draft enjoined us to do: "forget differences of race, language and religion".

Forget — meaning erase, extinguish, expunge, obliterate differences of race, language and religion? Can that be possible?

How does one forget differences of language, for instance? Every time I hear a Chinese Singaporean speak Mandarin or Hokkien, I am bound to remember, not forget, that I do not know Mandarin or Hokkien, and that these languages produce world-views quite different from the languages I am acquainted with. And as for forgetting differences among religions, who but an agnostic could have taken that as a serious possibility?

The formulation in the Pledge as we know it — "one united people, regardless of race, language or religion" — is more realistic in its command. It does not deny racial, linguistic or religious differences exist, let alone call for their obliteration. Rather, we are enjoined to go beyond them.

"Remember we are different — and then accept our plurality, set aside our differences, go beyond them," the Pledge urges. That is difficult enough but far more possible than: "Forget our differences — and then make sure you never remember them, erase all memory of our plurality", as the first draft would have demanded of us.

Sometimes, we have to remember our differences in order to go beyond them — as when we make provisions for minority representation in Parliament, for instance. We could have said racial differences don't matter, let us forget them, no need for a Presidential Council for Minority Rights, no need for minority representation in Parliament. And of course if the electorate had then elected only Chinese to Parliament, we would have discovered racial distinctions did matter after all, for the minorities would most certainly have felt excluded.

In the US, the courts have insisted on electoral districts with built-in African–American or Hispanic majorities to ensure minority representatives in legislatures. In Singapore, minorities are more or less evenly distributed throughout the island — so there are no majority Malay or Indian constituencies, and the Constitution guarantees minority representation in Parliament through group representation constituencies.

It remains to be seen which is the better system, but both share a similar recognition: You cannot get *E Pluribus Unum* — out of many, one — by simply denying that there are many.

"We, as citizens of Singapore, pledge ourselves to forget differences of race, language and religion" or "We, the citizens of Singapore, pledge ourselves as one united people, regardless of race, language or religion". By choosing the latter, Singapore's founding leaders recognised that we cannot be One without also acknowledging that we are Many, any more than one can produce a rainbow by smudging the different colours.

This is the first and most important thing we should note about the "we" in our Pledge: It does not call for the erasure of differences. We are not enjoined to forget our separate identities. Rather, we are urged to accept our plurality. And we are urged to go beyond them — go beyond our separate racial, linguistic, religious, cultural identities, so as to encompass the imagined community that lies beyond our differences.

Becoming Singaporean, in other words, from the beginning, was never conceived as a matter of subtraction but rather of addition; not a matter of less but of more; not a matter of forgetting our separate identities but of remembering the possibility of a national identity beyond those separate identities.

It is difficult in retrospect to piece together what happened in those six months, between February 1966 (when Mr Rajaratnam penned the first draft of the Pledge) and August 1966 (when we first recited the Pledge as we know it), but somehow our founding leaders — perhaps unknown to themselves, perhaps tentatively — began imagining in those months the possibility of a national Singaporean identity, and became firmer in their conviction that Singapore shall indeed "forever be a sovereign democratic and independent nation", as the Proclamation declares.

For the meaning of the Pledge — the meaning of "we" — was not obvious from the start. The Pledge itself was not the National Pledge as we now call it from the word go. Indeed, it wasn't till 1987 that the Pledge even featured in the National Day Parade, when an extended version of the song, *We Are Singapore*, was sung as the grand finale, together with the recitation of the Pledge. And it was not till 1988 that we recited the Pledge with the right fist clenched to the heart, as we do now; before that we raised our right hand as when taking an oath — as indeed the Pledge was initially conceived, an oath taken by schoolchildren before the flag.

The meaning of the Pledge, in other words — the meaning of "we" — accrued as the story of our island-nation unfolded. As we became more confident that a Singaporean national identity was not only possible but was beginning to take shape, the "we" became more substantial and the Pledge became a more powerful statement of our ideals.

It was the future of our own elaboration that imbued our originating symbols and ideals with meaning; our history did not unfold like a macadamised road from our originating symbols and ideals. It was our commitment to the possibility of a national identity — We, the citizens of Singapore — that produced the "we"; we did not begin with a fully conscious "we" that came festooned with a ready-made national identity.

And so should it be over the next 50, 100, 1,000 years: Every moment in our as a yet-to-unfold tale must begin with the decision: We shall exist.

It must always be possible to say "we, the citizens of Singapore"; that the elaboration of a "we" does not require the obliteration of differences — racial, religious or linguistic; that we accept our pluralities — political and social; that becoming a more perfect "we" or acquiring a deeper national identity, shall always be a matter of becoming more than the sum of our parts, not less, addition, not subtraction.

Singapore will undoubtedly face many challenges in its future — political, social, economic. In politics, we will have to learn to accommodate a demand for plurality, for a contest of ideas, for alternative views to be represented in Parliament. In society, we will have to learn to manage new diversities aside from the traditional ones of race, language and religion. In economics, we will have to strive to contain stark differences of income and wealth, and ensure that no part of "we" is left behind.

It was an incredibly brave thing that our founding generation did 50 years ago. The notion that a collection of such diverse peoples could have anything in common was indeed "ludicrous".

But just as God said in Genesis: "Let there be light, and there was light", our founding generation made a decision to exist — "We, the citizens of Singapore" — and so we came into existence. But unlike the "fiat lux", this is a decision that has to be repeated over and over again, emphatically, or "we" literally shall cease to exist.

Acknowledgements

IPS is grateful to the following institutions for their support of Singapore Perspectives 2016.

Keppel Corporation

a-reit
ascendas

Managed by Ascendas Funds Management (S) Limited
a member of Ascendas-Singbridge Group

ntuc Enterprise

TEMASEK

wilmar

Supported by

Supported by

SMU
SINGAPORE MANAGEMENT
UNIVERSITY

SINGAPORE
POLYTECHNIC | SP

Singtel

SUTD
SINGAPORE UNIVERSITY OF
TECHNOLOGY AND DESIGN

Established in collaboration with MIT

Temasek
POLYTECHNIC

Supported in-kind by

Raffles City
Convention Centre

Introduction

JUSTIN LEE AND TENG SIAO SEE

In 2015, Singapore celebrated 50 years of independence and we took stock of how the choices we made have gotten us to where we are. We also celebrated our achievements and started a conversation about the road ahead. With so much of our nation-building efforts premised upon the existence of this imagined community known as "Singapore", it is an opportune moment to question and reimagine who "we" are. We know what our aspirations are, but should our aspirations and ideals remain constant?

With the strong mandate given to the PAP government in the 2015 elections, what better way to contemplate these issues than to hear directly from our fourth generation of political leadership?

The Institute of Policy Studies (IPS) has pulled off a conference and logistics *tour de force* by successfully securing not one or two, but four distinguished members of our new generation leaders for this conference. Heng Swee Keat, Minister for Finance; Chan Chun Sing, Minister in Prime Minister's Office; Ng Chee Meng, then Acting Minister for Education (Schools); and Ong Ye Kung, then Acting Minister for Education (Higher Education and Skills) all came as speakers to share their vision of who we are, and their vision of our future.

Audience participation is important to IPS conferences and we have previously experimented with debates and audience voting in order to engage more people. For this January 2016 conference, we decided to try a new format of engagement. Instead of crowding up the session with multiple presenters, we had the Ministers deliver a concise formal speech on the theme of their panel. This gave our new leaders an opportunity to articulate their vision, values and ideas, but also more time for public engagement. For each

1

session, we assembled panellists made up of public servants, academics, community and corporate leaders who were given the task of asking our Ministers tough questions — questions that Singaporeans would want to ask but may not have an opportunity to. The purpose was to generate a lively discussion as we collectively clarify, challenge and refine the vision articulated. After the panellists raised key concerns and questions, there was a full half-hour for audience Q&A session so that more could participate in a dialogue with the Ministers on issues that matter to them.

In the first session, titled "Collaborative Governance?", Minister Chan Chun Sing explicated how good governance can ensure Singapore's competitive advantage given its demographic and resource constraints relative to larger nations. He defined good governance as a system of policies, products, processes and people that delivers better lives and livelihoods and a better future for Singaporeans. Minister Chan further elaborated that better governance should achieve these key principles, "ADAM": *alignment* of citizens with broad values and goals, faster *decision*-making and collective action, *acting* decisively, and *managing* and resolving consequences effectively. Questions pertaining to the wider participation in agenda co-creation and transparency of such processes were posed by the panellists and audience members. Minister Chan responded that tripartism such as that illustrated by the Inter-Religious Organisation (IRO) is an example of how partnership between and collective action from stakeholders is valued by the state, and that the quality of outcomes is not restricted by constructive close-door discussions. The issues of censorship and greater tolerance towards dissenting views, a reduced role of the state in society, provision of space for the development of a responsible and robust civil society, were also raised in this session.

In the second panel, "Cohesive Diversity?", Acting Minister Ng Chee Meng explored how Singapore could remain a harmonious and open society amid changing demographics and greater population diversification. He positioned diversity as a neutral term; it can be a source of strength or division. Cohesive diversity depends on both ideation and action and inclusive politics is crucial in finding balance amid the diversity. Noting increased inter-racial marriages and immigration, growing income inequality, and even the emerging varied causes Singaporeans are championing, Minister Ng pointed out that the challenge is to not leave anyone behind and respect all differences as the approach to diversity is refined. Panellists and the audience probed the Minister on the continued relevance of the existing CMIO (Chinese-Malay-Indian-Others) ethnic categories in the face of greater diversity and questioned the inclusivity of the Special Assistance Plan (SAP) schools. They also raised concerns over the need to educate Singaporeans on the society's religious diversity and wondered if policies differentiating citizens and non-citizens posed challenges to the integration of new citizens, PRs and foreigners.

For the third panel, "Inclusive Growth?" Minister Ong Ye Kung discussed how economic growth can be compatible with a more equitable and inclusive society through the use of progressive taxation, social transfers and a quality educational system (including continuing education) that levels the playing field. He cited the progress that Singapore has made, while panellists and audience members raised questions about the ability of various policy instruments in achieving economic growth (pointing to low labour productivity and innovation outputs) as well as social outcomes (pointing to poverty, rising inequality and cost of living). Ideas to reduce inequality were discussed, and went beyond income distribution to the distribution of benefits on the consumption side — such as single mothers and the LGBT community as minority groups that the state should pay more attention to in public housing subsidies, a kind of indirect transfer that creates parity in the ability of Singaporeans to purchase a home. Despite disagreements on how well Singapore was doing, there was general agreement on the approach that Singapore is taking — that we cannot afford social redistributions without economic growth. The panellists recognised that balancing growth and equity will often be a difficult trade-off. The negative impact on social integration that led to cut backs on foreign manpower is illustrative of such trade-offs. To make such decisions, Minister reminded Singaporeans to deal with it pragmatically, beyond ideological positions.

In the final panel, Minister Heng Swee Keat explored whether Singaporeans should reimagine who "We" are and how to move ahead as a people towards SG100 a session titled "The Future of 'We'". He discussed how the hope and aspirations of Singaporeans have changed, from merely survival to a life of purpose and to make a difference. Given globalisation and technology, national borders also become less relevant and people have to adapt to the flow of people and culture, creating questions for how we craft our national identity and achieve solidarity in light of new forms of diversity. He reiterated that the state should be a neutral arbiter in such issues and that more dialogue can help create mutual understanding between diverse groups in society. Panellists also asked Minister Heng for his views on the threat of terrorism, whether there can be more freedom of information, and LGBT issues, hoping to get a glimpse of his personal vision and values.

After the rich discussions of the conference, to keep the conversations going, we provided the panellists the option to pen their post-conference reflections. Those contributions have been included alongside the conference proceedings in this publication.

Collaborative Governance?

Chairperson:
Warren Fernandez, Editor, *The Straits Times*

Speaker:
Chan Chun Sing (CCS), Secretary-General, National Trades Union
Congress

Panel:
Lee Huay Leng (LHL), Editor, *Lianhe Wanbao*

Eugene Tan (ET), School of Law, Singapore Management University

Kok Heng Leun (KHL), Artistic Director, Drama Box Ltd

Chairperson: Morning, everyone. My name is Warren Fernandez and I'm
Editor of *The Straits Times*, and I think we are all ready for the first panel
discussion after that very stirring speech by Janadas [Devan]. It doesn't feel
very "we" up here — with the Minister there and the panellists here. I asked
Janadas about it and he said it's largely because of the camera angle. So we
have television to blame for that. But I think it's appropriate to start the
discussion with governance and politics, because that's how we would deliver
the idea of "we" — how we would govern ourselves. And the conference
theme starts simply — just one word, "we"; but then we go down from there
to "collaborative governance", which is a bit of a mouthful. If you know I'm
a newspaper man, and we like to simplify things, so for the purpose of this
discussion I'm just going to call it "good politics".

And calling it good politics puts our discussion in the context of some recent developments. First of all, you would have recollected the speech by President Tony Tan on Friday in Parliament where he talked about the importance of giving good policies, but also good politics. And I think it's important for us to get a good understanding going forward what we mean by good politics. I think the first thing to be said about good politics is that it doesn't mean no politics in Singapore, where we all somehow agree with everything the People's Action Party (PAP) or the government comes up with. But to be fair to the President in his speech, he did say that good politics means having checks and balances and stabilisers in the system; having ways for alternative views to surface and be incorporated in policies; having assurances to the minorities that they have a place in policymaking and the national life of Singapore. So I think it will be a good point of discussion for us today to get into the meat of what we mean by good politics and how we are going to get it.

But I also want to refer you to a second speech, which was made last week by another President — by the United States President Barack Obama in his final State of the Union address to the American Congress. And I'd like to quote a chunk of that speech for those of you who haven't heard it or read it, because I think a lot of it is relevant to our discussion today. To quote, the President Obama says this:

> *The future we want, all of us want, opportunity and security for our families, a rising standard of living, a sustainable, peaceful planet for our kids, all that is within reach. But it will only happen if we work together. It will only happen if we have rational, constructive debates, and will only happen if we fix our politics. A better politics doesn't mean we have to agree on every-thing. Our founding fathers expected us to argue, just as they did, fiercely. But democracy does require basic bonds of trust between its citizens. It doesn't work if we think the people who disagree with us are all motivated by malice. It doesn't work if we think that our political opponents are unpatriotic and trying to weaken the country. Democracy grinds to a halt without the willingness to compromise, or when even basic facts are contested, or we listen only to those who agree with us. Our public life withers when only the most extreme voices can hold the attention. And most of all,*

democracy breaks down when the average person feels their voice doesn't matter.

I cite this long quote because I think much of it is relevant to our discussion today, on getting good politics. And to discuss this issue we have a very distinguished and diverse panel. First, on my right, Minister Chan Chun Sing, NTUC (National Trades Union Congress) Secretary-General and Minister for the Prime Minister's Office. For this audience, you need no further introductions. You know how he was Chief of the Army, one of the rising stars after the 2011 election, and one of the key members of the fourth generation of leadership for the country.

On my left, we have my old comrade-in-arms, Lee Huay Leng, a political commentator for many years, and now Editor of *Lianhe Wanbao*; and another political watcher, Associate Professor Eugene Tan, Law Lecturer at the Singapore Management University. And last but certainly not least, Kok Heng Leun, Artistic Director of Drama Box and I am sure he will express the views of practitioners in the artistic community. But first, let us give time to the Minister for his thoughts on the topics of good government, good politics, or if you must, collaborative governance.

CCS: Thank you, Warren. Now that Warren has changed the topic, we will probably need to invent a new sharing on the fly. But Warren is right. Whatever you call it, whether you call it collaborative governance, governance or good politics, it will come back down to a few similar things.

Today I will start with a real story that I will share with many of you. Not too long ago, I was speaking to a group of international mid-level executives undergoing a programme. They came to Singapore and I asked for their views on where they would invest — where they would put their money — in 15 years, 30 years and in 50 years.

Almost all of them chose the US, China, Indonesia, India and so forth. I was even more interested to find out their reasons. And they inevitably spoke about demography and resources being the two main considerations. And I thought to myself, if resources and demography define destiny, then there's very little chance for Singapore to survive in the next 50 years or even less. But I asked them, "If resources and demographics are defining factors in today's world, then who would be the superpower?"

The point I was trying to share with them was simply this: That I think, we think, in Singapore, governance — good governance — can create the special competitive advantage for us to remain as an independent, free and successful country — as [one that] can defy the odds of history; that a small city state like us can survive and thrive.

Then, as Warren says, if this is so important to us, what then defines good governance?

To me, it simply means two things. One, it must lead to better lives and livelihoods for all Singaporeans. Two, I think it must lead to a better future for Singapore. So, for Singaporeans and for Singapore. Good governance, collaborative governance. Sounds like a good thing, feels like a good thing, smells like a good thing. So why is it not happening more often than it [should]?

It was the same in my conversation last year when I visited the International Labour Organization. Tripartism was a good thing — [that] was the official doctrine. Everybody wants it but few are able to achieve it. So the question is why? There are a few reasons for us to want to make sure that we have good governance. Good governance can be defined as having a good product, good policies, good processes and good people.

I start with the first "**P**": Product or policies. It must lead to outcomes that enable us to better the lives of citizens and leave behind a better Singapore for future generations. That is, to me, good product. Second, it must have a good process that engages the collective wisdom, power and energies of our people for collective action. And for those of you familiar with the military's OODA loop[1], whereby people say that whoever can respond earlier [or] faster will beat the enemy. In governance, there is a similar loop. I call it the ADAM loop. Whoever can **a**lign the goals, the values and objectives of his people better; whoever can **d**ecide faster for today and tomorrow; whoever can **a**ct collectively [and] decisively; and whoever can **m**anage the consequences and adjust resolutely will be the better model of governance. And it is a continuous cycle. It will go on and on. So as a process, whoever can align its people better (shared values, shared goals, shared objectives); whoever can decide faster, decide better, not just for this generation but for the next as well; whoever can act collectively,

---

[1] OODA refers to "observe, orient, decide, and act".

harnessing the power of all its people; and whoever can manage the consequences and make the necessary adjustments as we go along better — to me, that's the process.

But ultimately, the third factor — people — is just as important. A good system is just not one that delivers good results today. A good system is not one that is just populated by good people today, but [one that] continuously brings forth even better people for tomorrow.

Many countries in history fail not because they don't have good leaders in that point in time. Many countries attained great heights because they have good leaders at a point in time. Our challenge is not just to be great at that point in time, like a flash in the pan. Our challenge is to continuously bring forth good people with the right values, with the right capabilities, with their heart in the right place, not for themselves but for the country so that we can continue to defy the odds of history and, as Janadas would say, that in time to come, we would still be able to say "we" proudly because "we" have that sense of identity, that sense of purpose, that sense of mission; that regardless of our diverse backgrounds, regardless of our diverse histories, we can look forward to a common future.

This is the kind of people that we hope to bring forward to serve Singapore and Singaporeans. So if you ask me what is good politics, good products, good policies, good processes and most importantly, good people — [it is] system that continuously bring forth good people.

But on the other hand, when we talk about collaborative governance, we hope that it will not degenerate into a situation whereby people just come forth to talk about what they want, and then either leave the execution to someone else, or to absolve their responsibilities to the future generation. I won't call that collaborative governance; I call that compromised governance. In many countries, we see compromised governance, where governance is defined by what some call it pork-barrel politics, where it goes down to the lowest common denominator where people are only concerned about who gets what at a certain point in time. And there is no concept of stewardship, of leaving behind something better for the next generation. Harnessing what we have in this generation to leave something behind for the next generation, while taking care of this generation.

We also do not want it to be a democracy of empty words. We do not just want to talk, but we want to act collectively. If we can do that, then even as a small country, I think we can defy the odds. But most importantly, in all that we do, we must not forget to take care of the current generation, bearing in mind the needs of the future generation. In all the conversations, it is always easy to talk about what this generation needs. But it is always hard to talk about what the next generation may need. Or for generations to come, what do they actually need.

And this is the reason why, building on the Our Singapore Conversation (OSC), going forward, when we start the SG Futures series of dialogues, we hope to go beyond conversation. We want to translate conversation into action where each and every Singaporean has a stake in building the future of ours.

And I often remind people — a perfect product given to us feels less than a slightly imperfect product that is collectively created by us, ourselves. And if we understand this, we will understand why it is so important, so powerful for us to go forward in the next 50 years, the next 100 years, to harness the collective ideas, aspirations and most important, actions of our people to build this country of ours.

So on that note, I will like to hear your ideas on how we can move forward as one people, not just in conversation but in action. Thank you very much.

Chairperson: Thank you, Minister. We want this session to be very inter-active and all about "we". And to get a good discussion going. So thank you for giving us an overview of the three "Ps" — Products and policies, processes and people. And we will come to that in a minute. First, let us get a quick reaction to the minister's talk from Huay Leng.

LHL: This collaborative government that we are talking about... actually, it's not something very new. We have been talking about this for many years actually, but using a different term. I remember Singapore 21, we then had a huge consultation on active citizenry, what Singaporeans want, that every-one matters and all that. And then until now we have OSC. So the number of participants that were consulted grew from 6,000 for Singapore 21 to OSC (the reported number was 47,000 or so).

So to you, how have we moved in terms of this collaborative governance, in terms of the qualitative change, not just the numbers we have grown in consultation? What do you actually value in this consultation? And also, comparing with... you mentioned good product, good process, good people.... But what is the definition of good? Your definition of good may not be the same as some people. And comparing with 2011 when you just came in, are we now, after last year's election, in a good state?

CCS: Okay, let me share my thoughts and build on Huay Leng's comment. First I think, actually when we talk about the concept of collaborative governance, I don't have in mind just things like SG Future, OSC, SG21 and so forth.

Actually, we have this model of collaborative governance in some parts of our society that have worked very well over many years, and I'll just give two examples. And I will then try to draw out from these two examples what I deem as the success factors. And I will use tripartism and the Inter-Religious Organisation (IRO) or the Inter-Racial and Religious Confidence Circle (IRCC). Because these two sets of issues share many positives attributes that I think we can pick out and expand to other areas in our society.

In order for this to work, first, there must be shared goals. Shared goals don't mean "my goals versus your goals". It's about our common goals. We all have our differences, we all have our preferences, we all have our objectives, but can we transcend that? As they say, if there is a thesis, there is an antithesis. Can we come to the synthesis? That's my favourite phrase. Can we come to the synthesis?

In tripartism and in the IRO work or the IRCC work, there is a common goal that transcends beyond the individual interest of the individual parties. The sum of the parts is actually greater than each individual in addition. And because of that, they have a shared goal; they have a shared value that makes it work. But most importantly, they trust each other. It took a long time for such mechanisms to come about, to build that level of trust over prolonged period, over many challenges and crises.

When you have trust, then we can talk about the next set of things, which is solution-seeking on how to build a better future. In collaborative governance, it is not just about sharing what we all want, it is not just about finding a solution we can all accept. But it is more importantly about acting collectively to take leadership for the decision that we have made collectively and to take responsibility for what we have done collectively.

So when something goes wrong in the tripartite relationship, each partner takes equal responsibility for what has happened and each of them takes it upon themselves to make it work. It is the same for the IRO or IRCC. They have a common vision; they want to make things work. They collaborate not just to define the problem, not just to seek the solution, but most importantly to take collective action and collective responsibility.

So to me, collaborative governance is not just at the conversation level of defining problems and solutions-seeking. It is more than that. It requires us to take collective action, collective responsibility and have the collective leadership. Easy to say, not easy to do because in this process, you will require trust, you will require respect and most importantly, it will require humility. Humility to say that each of us may have our own perspective but each of us may not have the best perspective. That each of us can learn to respect each other's views, build on each other's views and then produce something even better for all the groups that we are in.

So to me — that will come to the second issue that Huay Leng mentioned — what is success? Success goes back to: Is the product or policy better? Is the outcome better? Is the process one that engages, one that energises the people? One that uplifts the people? And in the process, do we groom another generation of people with the same values, same ethos to want to do even better? So to me, that will be success.

Chairperson: Sir, if I can jump in, I take your point about the need for shared goals and trust. I think tripartism is an interesting example because it does deliver on the good policies and the good outcomes that you are talking about. But one criticism of tripartism that is often made in Singapore is that the process often takes place behind closed doors and much of the debate, the exchange of views and compromise, isn't quite seen. So, many people think that there isn't that robust exchange of views. So I think that's what Huay Leng is alluding to, how do you go about making sure that there is a qualitative change in that process?

CCS: So I think we take a very practical approach to these issues. It doesn't mean that the tripartite partners have no disagreement amongst themselves.

And it'll be odd, weird even if the tripartite partners do not have different perspectives.

But the question is, what will allow us to have a better outcome? Open debates work sometimes, closed-door consultations work at other times. We must be able to use both processes and other processes to engage our people. Even though it might be closed-door, it doesn't mean that it's a monolithic discussion. It doesn't mean that the union leaders or the government officials or the employers for that matter, all have the same views.

Whether it is open or closed discussions, what's most important is that people come to the table with a shared goal of making the future better for our country and our workers. They have the same values of respect, trust and humility. And most importantly, they want to find a better solution not just for themselves but for all those involved. So I can also assure that even amongst the union leaders, they would have disagreements. Even amongst the employers, and even sometimes the government officials, they would have different perspectives, even within the same block of constituents as you say. But that doesn't prevent us from seeking a robust solution that meets the needs of everyone and the country. So I think, to me, that's important. The form we can tweak, the form we may use it differently, in different context, depending on the issues. But the substance of what we do must not change.

Chairperson: Okay, let's draw Eugene [Tan], a former nominated MP to the process as well. Eugene, please.

ET: Thank you, Warren. Thank you, Minister. When I first learnt of the topic of collaborative governance for this panel, I was quite puzzled because it struck me very much as an oxymoron. For good and effective governance, governance has to be collaborative. After all, governance is very much about trying to get people on board to attain the governance objectives and challenges of the day. This often requires building bridges to people who may not agree with you. And when you consider collaborative governance, in light of what the President had said at the opening of the 13th Parliament, we might now be going into a situation where we have the adjectives trying to do the work of nouns.

So for example, we have this binary of good and bad politics, collaborative and non-collaborative governance. I think we all agree on the importance of collaborative governance. The key question then is, how do we get there? Of course, we have good examples. You have pointed out tripartism as one. You would be very familiar with other examples of collaborative governance in Singapore such as the People's Association. Here, the basic idea is about reaching out to and engaging different segments of the population through grassroots organisations. The importance of that shared purpose is clear. But, increasingly, it is shared values that would make the vital difference. In this regard, how we achieve the desired governance outcomes matters a lot more.

We have almost finessed collaborative governance; look at the trade unions, the grassroots organisations sector. They are all very intimately tied to the ruling party. My question is: In the event that the ruling party becomes incompetent or corrupt, something which even the founding Prime Minister Lee Kuan Yew didn't rule out, how do we prevent Singapore from going through a systemic collapse? In such a scenario, when you have all these key levers of power and mobilisation severely compromised, then trust and confidence in key institutions and organisations will not be there.

Chairperson: Minister, before you respond, can I first get Kok Heng Leun's views as well. Then you can respond to both of them together. Heng Leun, you want to jump in?

KHL: Thank you, Minister. Thank you, Warren. I'll put across some observations first so that then Minister can maybe respond to the observations. I take the 3Ps, I take from process, then I look at people, then I look at the product. Because I believe that if we do not get the due process, the product means nothing. If you do not know who you're working with, and who is actually leading, again, the product means nothing.

So I am going to look at the process and then reflect on what Janadas has actually spoken about. Just now about "we" as citizens, which was what S. Rajaratnam has said. I think the line "We, the citizens of Singapore" is very interesting, because we start to look at Singaporeans now whereby we have multiple allegiances. We are not really talking about ourselves as citizens of Singapore, but we see ourselves as a very globalised society where we actually then have allegiance to different things. That's the first thing that came to my mind.

Secondly, of course, in our pledge, we talk about race, religion, culture and language. But at the same time, the society has become more diverse. Then when we define ourselves as an individual, we are no longer defining ourselves based on those four simple categories. We are looking at gender, social class and many other things. So that's the second thing.

So in the due process of doing collaborative governance, how do you actually achieve diversity? If I look at the new future economy committee, the surprising element here is that as I am looking through, the Steering Committee is headed by mainly business people. And we are looking at a kind of complex society right now where when we want to look at [the] economy, we really want to look at it — how is it going to be sustainable? And to be sustainable, we probably have to look at it from the environmental, social, as well as in terms of the geographical [angles]. So these are the few things we have to look at. However, the committee does not reflect such diversity. Where are the anthropologists who are very important in the discussion of culture? In fact, we have now gone into a society whereby we are not just talking about economics as the main driving force. In fact, culture becomes a very important aspect of learning how to achieve a kind of sustainable society.

I think the next thing I want to talk about is the people. When we are talking about leadership, especially in collaborative governance, are the leaders able to let go of the power to say that "I am not setting the agenda but the agenda can be negotiated"? Secondly, in terms of administration of policies, would public servants be strong enough or even confident enough to work collectively? Because in collective working, you know... one feels as if one is giving up one's power. Third, then the policies — how sustainable are the policies? We shall come back to that point again, just now. So these are the three different things that are in my mind. So I'll like the Minister to respond.

Chairperson: But if I could sum up, broadly speaking, we are talking about an increasingly diverse population and electorate. And how do we structure our processes and systems to address that greater diversity and plurality?

CCS: Let me build on Eugene's point first. Actually, I have to totally agree with Eugene. When I was first given this topic on collaborative governance, I was just wondering, "Is there governance that is non-collaborative?" Then I thought about it and said, yeah… actually there are three types of governance historically, two of which are non-collaborative in the true sense of the word.

First, non-collaborative governance means probably monarchies, autocracies… you know… just one person decides. So that's not a good example, that's not where we want to go. The second type is what I call pseudo-democracy, whereby different groups with different interests come together for a negotiated settlement. To me, that's also not very uplifting. That really is not collaborative governance; it's just about interest groups coming together. Then there is the third possibility, which is the idealised Athenian democracy. I say idealised because even in Athens, they never achieved it, whereby [there is] collective wisdom and power and actions of all *for* the good of all. That is what we strive to attain.

I won't say that we are there. It is a work in progress but there are certainly many things that we can do much more of, along that line. And the concern that Eugene raised is actually our same concern. On the one hand, we know we are small, we need to be united, we need to get our act together, we need to move fast. And yet when we want to be united, move fast, how do we make sure that we are not blind-sided at the same time? That is always the tension.

On the other hand, if we are all quarrelling with each other every day, we can't move fast and we won't survive very well. That is the inherent tension. So if anything, I think what I have seen from this government and the previous generations of leaders, they are much more concerned about these issues than many of us would think they are.

And that is the reason why we always ask ourselves institutionally, how do we make sure that we bring in people with diverse perspectives? How do we design a system whereby there are stabilisers in the system — that even as we do the good things, we must constantly check ourselves at which point a good policy or good things have reached its limit, needs to be changed, needs to be adjusted? How do we know that there are enough stabilisers even as we are moving fast? So we have the same concern, more than anybody else.

Because our concern is not whether the PAP will rule forever; our larger concern is whether Singapore will last forever. That is our concern. Political parties are there to lead, but political parties must evolve in order to make sure that the higher goal of sustaining this country of ours is achieved, that we continue to defy the odds of history. And that is what we are out to do.

Heng Leun's point is precisely the challenge that we are grappling with — multiple identities, multiple allegiances. But having said that, I also don't think that this is an entirely new problem. In fact, in the early years of our independence, we also had the same problems in other ways.

I remember my grandmother used to save every single cent in order to send back S$50, which was quite a lot of money, back to China at that point in time. She would want to be buried back in China. And I am sure many of our forefathers would have gone through that path as well. But the new kinds of identities that we have now are perhaps a bit different.

Some youngsters ask, "Why should I be a citizen of any country?" I can be an employee of Google, Microsoft… whose GDP is probably as big as yours. And if I'm a Citibanker, maybe I'm more recognised than many others and so forth. These are the kind of competing and conflicting identities that we have to grapple with. And many people who have come through Singapore, succeeded through the Singapore system, have gone on to other places to bring up their families and future generations. And we wish them well.

The question is, for every Singaporean who is still here, for everyone who has come through Singapore, as they go through our system, will they continue to support the values that we stand for? That Singapore, being an artificial country in many senses of the word, we are not defined by a common past, we are not defined by a common ancestry, a common language, common religion, common race and so on and so forth. But that we can always be united by a common destiny, a common future based on a set of common values. If we can reach that stage, then I would argue that we have something even more powerful than those many nations that depend on common ancestry, common race, language and religion.

There are very few countries in the world that define their national identity based on the future. Most countries, most nations in the world define their identity based on the past, common ancestry, common language, common culture. But we have also seen for those countries that try to define their future based on a common set of values, they are also and they can also be very attractive to the people around the world. So this is where we are. We will have to continue to grapple with this national identity building.

In the last 50 years, our economic success has bought us time. Is it sufficient? It's too early to say. Are we there yet? Probably not. Are we closer today than yesterday? Definitely yes. Will we continue to progress down this path? I think we will because we have the basis to go forward. We are in a much better position than in 1965 when we talked about a sense of national identity. In 1965, I think very few would dare to say that we should even dare to dream of a national identity, that our people were defined by a set of values, a set of ethos that bind us together regardless of race, language and religion. And we will have to continue to try this, to build on this, even though different identities are pulling us apart.

Just a short response to conversation about the Committee for the Future Economy. Actually, there are people there who are not just there because of their business credentials. And in fact, we are very aware that in order for us to have a strong conversation, a useful conversation, the economic considerations cannot be divorced from the social considerations and other multi-faceted issues including culture and so forth.

Because as we grow the economy, it is not just an end in itself, it's also a means. A means for us to provide a better livelihood for our people. A means for us to grow the sense of identity that we can be proud of ourselves as Singaporeans, that despite our resource limitations, despite our demographic challenges, we can defy the odds because we can have good governance, good leadership, good system, to prove to people that we are worth their investment. We are worth them paying attention to us.

And then the last point if I may just add is the negotiated agenda that Heng Leun mentioned. And this is the part I agree with. Every party, regardless of its government, individuals, private sector and so forth, we must have the confidence to go into a conversation to say, "Let's define the problem together." And not just defining the problem, let's find the solution. If we can do that well, it's even more empowering. We need to learn the art of having diverse people come together and say, "Let's define the issues together, let's define our collective goals and the rules we will abide by." This is what I call alignment.

If we do this well, the second part, the decision-making, the solution-seeking, is much simpler. And I always say, coming from the military, if you want to take an objective, you can go by the left or you can go by the right. It matters less if you go by the left or you go by the right, but it matters most that we all go together. Don't let us have some going to the left, some going to the right, and the rest staying here. That will be a disaster for Singapore.

Now having decided — coming back to ADAM — having decided, then we need to act collectively. But if we have the initial alignment of our common goals, objectives and shared values, then acting in unison is straightforward. We can have the best decision but if we do not have the common goals and common objectives, acting in unison is difficult. And then, last but not least, we have to take collective responsibilities. We must not end up in a situation where having decided, having acted upon it, if something goes wrong, then it's somebody else's fault. As some people told me, success has many parents, but failure is an orphan. It shouldn't be that.

QUESTION AND ANSWER SESSION

Chairperson: Can I jump in at this point, Minister, because I do want to get the audience into the conversation as well so that this is really a conversation for "we". I think we are in agreement at this stage, on the 3Ps. Getting the policies right, getting the processes right, getting the people right. I think we are still grappling with this. How to do that? Can I get questions from the floor? Just raise your hand, tell us who you are, and keep your question short so that we can discuss it. I see a gentleman there at the back. Please go ahead.

Q1: Good morning, my name is Paul Tambyah from the School of Medicine, NUS. I think I'm also one of the few token representatives of the alternative parties here. My question is actually directed at the Minister. And I think these are very good points that you have brought up. My question is a little bit more fundamental. And the question is actually, when we talk about governance, the question is, who is this governance for? I thought it's very interesting that you brought up the idea about the investors. And I think I speak to many Singaporeans who feel that very often, the perception — it may be wrong, is that, governance is for the benefit of the investors, whereas… there are academics within the institution that hosts this meeting who did a very good study about Singaporean attitudes to emigration a few years ago. And they showed that one in four young Singaporeans is actively thinking of migrating from Singapore. So my question is: Do you think they should try to address this question of what is the purpose of governance? Is it for the investor, or is it for the one in four Singaporeans who are actively trying to get out of Singapore in the next five years. Thank you.

CCS: Very simple. I think I have answered that. The purpose of governance is to, one, for better lives and livelihoods of our people; and two, to be good stewards, to leave behind a better Singapore for the next generation. There will be some who might leave us, and there will be others who will come.

The question is, for the bulk of the Singaporeans here, are their lives better today than yesterday? That is what keeps us awake each and every day. For every one that might leave us for some reasons, will there be others who will be attracted to our values, our models? No country in the world is in the position to say that all that it does is policies, is structures to attract everyone. And some people would self-select. But even those people who leave us, do they believe in our models, our values, our systems? The very same values and systems that they have benefited through. For others who want to come and join us, do they come here for economic reasons only, or initially? Having come here, would they continue to reinforce the very values that have put us in good stead till now? Will they continue to grow our system and our values? If we can do that, then I think we can quite safely say that we have at least succeeded to a certain extent.

Chairperson: Can I ask the panellists to please feel free to jump in if you have questions or thoughts as well, so we get a conversation? I like to follow up on that question by asking a political question, which is the way in which we choose to organise governance must reflect the views of the electorate surely? And how people feel they want to be governed. And if you look at the last two elections, in the 2011 election which was widely seen as a setback for the ruling party, many said that the opposition was in the ascendant and people were drawing straight lines into the future where we will have a two-party state. The last election in 2015, the PAP did very well. They got 69.9% of the votes. I'd like to get a sense of how you read that 69.9% because after 2011, there was a lot of talk about us in Singapore, of being in a "new-normal". So what happens after 2015? Are we back to the old-normal? Are we in a new new-normal? Because how you interpret that result will in a way shape how you respond to it. So it'll be very interesting, I think, for all of us here to get a sense from you minister, as a younger key member of the younger team. How you think of the views of the electorate, on how they want to be governed?

CCS: I am not exactly sure of the definition of the new-normal and the old-normal because when I talk to different people, they all have different perspectives. But if I talk to my residents on the ground, as I visit them each and every week, their needs are very simple. They are concerned about things like, "Has my life become better compared to yesterday? The week before, the month before, the year before?" "Are my children going to have a better future than me?" "Will we leave behind a better system, a better future for my children?" Two very simple and basic, and perhaps funda-mental questions — and any government that can answer these two questions well, get its process right, I think, will earn the trust of its people.

Any government that cannot answer these two questions well, cannot deliver on these two, will not earn the votes of its people regardless of how eloquent it might be. And I think Singaporeans are practical people. They look for leadership to overcome the many challenges ahead of us. They look for leaders with the right values to take the country forward. And so long as the government, this government or any other government, abides by this rule to make sure that the livelihoods of our people are continuously taken care of, that we will leave behind a better future for the next generation. Then I think the voters will take care of the results in every election for us.

Having said that, we also understand that as society becomes more diverse, there will be greater desire for the plurality of views to be heard. And incidentally, this is the reason why this government, the PAP government, has instituted the Nominated Member of Parliament (NMP) system and the Non-Constituency Member of Parliament (NCMP) system from the position of strength, as I would call it.

Why? Because it does not need to if it doesn't want to listen to alternative opinions. In every election, at the start of the election, we are guaranteed that at least 15–20% of the seats in Parliament will be populated by non-PAP, non-establishment people. Because even assuming the PAP wins all 89 seats, there will minimally be nine NCMPs and another nine NMPs — 18 altogether. So that's perhaps about 15% of the entire Parliament. Why do we do this innovation? Is it, as some suspect, perhaps a safety valve? No, I don't think so. It is because we recognise that to govern well and to meet the aspirations of our people, [we need] greater plurality of views. We are prepared, we are confident that we should allow and institutionalise in our system this plurality of views.

Having said that, it doesn't mean that the 89 or 80 odd PAP candidates are all monolithic. They all have their views, they all have their perspectives. If they are monolithic, they are only monolithic in one aspect. And that is that they want a better future for Singaporeans and Singapore. All else can be discussed, all else can be negotiated — but the unifying factor must be that people who get into Parliament, regardless whether it is a PAP candidate or opposition candidate or NCMP or NMP, we must be united by this aim to do better, given our finite resources, given our circumstances, to deliver a better future for Singapore and Singaporeans.

Chairperson: Anybody from the panel wants to jump in? Eugene as a former NMP? Please go ahead.

ET: I won't speak about the NMP scheme though. I think the discussion so far demonstrates the tendency for us to get into binaries. So we have good and bad politics, constructive and destructive politics. Then we have the foreigners versus the Singaporeans, practical and idealistic politics.

Even as we focus on governance outcomes, we mustn't ignore the processes. The Minister did talk about processes. If we take care of the processes, I think we can be assured of better outcomes. But when we go into binaries, then anything that doesn't fall into good politics is, by definition, bad politics. Anything that is not practical gets thrown out of the window.

Many young people today continue to be idealistic. Despite growing up in a fairly comfortable lap of luxury, they do care about idealism. After all, it was idealism that inspired us and brought us to where we are today, starting from our independence in 1965.

Chairperson: Can I take another question from the floor, please? Professor [Tommy] Koh.

Q2: Mr Chairman, since we are still in the month of January, may I wish everybody happy new year. I would like to thank Minister Mr Chan Chun Sing for his opening remarks. They are very good and I agree with all of them. I think in Singapore, we do enjoy good governance. Our system of governance is characterised by transparency, inclusiveness and integrity. So we have a good system.

Minister Chan, I hope you will not mind if I ask you two provocative questions. The PAP is probably the most successful political party in the world. But it is a victim of its own success. A former Minister George Yeo has once compared the PAP to a banyan tree — the banyan tree has such a huge canopy that it doesn't allow things to grow under its shadow. So he spoke of the need to trim the banyan tree. This was, I think in 1991, in his lecture on civic society. So my question to you is, if the party is aware and acknowledges the need to trim the banyan tree further in the new Singapore? Would the party give more room to civic society, to civil society, and reduce the role that it plays?

I give you an example. I am often puzzled by the fact that so many PAP MPs are leading various sporting organisations, even though some of them don't seem to have any obvious sporting credentials. So why doesn't the PAP trust the people and allow people who are sportsmen and sportswomen who have excelled in these sports, but who are also men and women of integrity, to lead those organisations? So that is my first question.

Second question, I am asking on behalf of Kok Heng Leun, who is probably too shy to ask you. There is some unhappiness in our artistic and cultural community in the past year. Two events I think caused a lot of unhappiness. A film produced by a very prominent and respected filmmaker was banned. And a book grant given by National Arts Council (NAC) was subsequently withdrawn. So my question to you, Minister Chan, is can we expect in the years to come, the continued growth of what I call, a culture of tolerance? Would the government embrace the continued growth of a culture of tolerance? A culture that respects and accepts diversity of points of view. A culture that accepts alternative views, even dissenting views, and does not seek to punish those who express these different views. Either by banning a film or withdrawing a book grant. I apologise if I have offended you.

CCS: I think these are very good questions to get the discussion into the meat. Perhaps I should answer Eugene's question and I think it would lead nicely into what Prof. Koh mentioned as well. I never see things in a binary form, good or bad. Some people think there are good policies and there are bad policies — and in the extreme, there are. But most policies lie somewhere in between. There are tradeoffs to be made. There are decisions to be made that will be most appropriate to the circumstances and the needs at the time. I share with you my own personal journey.

After 2011, I was very, very saddened by what I call slogan politics. The 2011 election had a lot of debates about very serious issues that concerned the future of our country: transport, housing, immigration and so forth. But what I was most saddened by was what I call slogan politics. Foreigners bad, Singaporeans good. Or Singaporeans bad, foreigners good. You know, how does that get us anywhere? And this was the reason, and this still is the reason why, till today, every month, when I'm in Singapore, I decide to hold an informal policy discussion, with groups of young people, to share with them. Policies are only good in context. We must understand when to adjust, when to change. There is no one policy that will be eternally relevant or appropriate. The good policymaker is one who knows when to adapt and adjust. And I hope that all Singaporeans will also share this philosophy. That as we go forth and look for solutions — better solutions to build a better Singapore, we must know the plethora of options out there. Pick the one that is most appropriate at that point in time, according to the needs of our circumstances, and be prepared to jettison those that are less relevant. Only so will we stay nimble and agile as a country. So, to me, I don't necessarily see things in a binary state. I see it as a continuum, and it is a judgment required at any point in time.

And I want to build on that to come to Prof. Koh's point. Yes, we are a victim of our success, because we have been so successful. And we also have expectations in society that, should anything go wrong, the government must come in to fix the problem and to arbitrate. Frankly speaking, if you are sitting on the government's side, how often you'll wish that you don't have to be the final arbiter for some of these things. On the sports association, it's very interesting, the history of how this came about. I think many of the MPs, unless they are already involved in the sport, would be asking themselves: Why do I need to do this in order to help the organisations to do better? Sometimes they are charged with the responsibilities because the sports organisation invites them, hoping they can make a contribution. And that must be the basis: Whether as an MP or not an MP, if you join an organisation and association, you must want, and you must be able to make a contribution. You cannot be there just as a figurehead, because it just destroys the trust in the system. So where the MP can value-add, yes by all means, go ahead and make a contribution, and if the sporting organisation decides for themselves that they want a particular MP as their patron or whatever position, and if they think they can make a contribution, yes, by all means do that, because for other MPs who are not involved, I mean they would have other preoccupations also. Take the Football Association for example. Whenever Singapore doesn't do well in soccer — sometimes this happens more often than we like — the question inevitably is: What is the government going to do about this mess? So we are caught in this situation, whether we like it or not, but does this mean that the government will have to solve every [part] of this problem? I would hope that somebody [could] come forth and take charge of the Football Association and bring it to greater heights, whether MP or not MP, whether sporting icon or not sporting icon — just somebody who can help us bring it to greater heights.

Having said that, coming to the next issue — and I mention about this, you know collaborative governance, collaborative leadership — is also about collective responsibility. Take the arts community for example. How we wish that the arts community will be able to settle amongst themselves, first and foremost, how to define areas, arts classification, what is permissible, what is good and so forth, and not only among the arts community, but also to convince the rest of Singapore and Singaporeans that that decision is right. And this is the reason why we have set up the NAC. We have set up many other councils, to harness the energy of the non-government people to give us advice, and share with us their perspectives on what is acceptable to society. So I think the issue is not so much as within the arts community deciding per se, the issue is also about the arts community convincing the rest of Singapore and Singaporeans. We don't want a situation whereby a particular community, be it the arts or another community, tells the government that this is what we think is correct, please go and convince the rest of the world. Now that is not collaborative governance. That is called passing the buck.

But on the other hand, you compare the IRO or the IRCC that you mentioned before. They decide on something, then they're prepared to say that, "I think this is the common space that we must defend, for the good of our country. And we as religious leaders, the inter-faith religious leaders, we will go out there and make a stand, to defend this common stance of ours, to defend the common space." I think that's good. I think we will like to see more of that. So when it comes to finding consensus across society, it is not easy. Every group, whether government or non-government, has the right and the responsibility to try to galvanise everybody. If we can do that, then we can truly achieve collaborative governance, which was why I started with the basic premise.

Collaborative governance is not just about everyone telling the government, or telling somebody else, what they want. Collaborative governance is not just about aggregating individual interests. For those of you who are familiar with game theory, you will even question whether the aggregation of individual interests necessarily leads to a superior national interest, whether each and every one of us pursuing our own interests — will we be caught in what they call the prisoner dilemma, and end up with a sub-optimal situation. So governance is not so straightforward. It is about alignment of our people's values and goals, doing that well, deciding, acting upon it, but most importantly, taking collective responsibility. And I will hope that one day, in these areas, as Prof. Koh mentioned, that the respective communities will take responsibility, ownership, not just within their community, but to go forth and convince the rest of Singapore and Singaporeans, why that position is best for our society, and I think that is the challenge, when it comes to many of these thorny issues.

Chairperson: Heng Leun, do you want to jump in on that point? I mean, rather than have Prof. Koh speak on your behalf.

KHL: Thank you, Prof., for raising those questions. I think the arts community is one of the most vibrant civil societies at work. I think what is interesting is [that] the community themselves are organising themselves to understand the problems that they're facing, or even to articulate issues and problems. In collaborative governance, I think it is alright for it to be chaotic. I think that's part of the premise of what it is. But to be chaotic doesn't mean that you will always end up in fights, and be unproductive. Actually it always ends up in you [getting to] understand each other better. I think when we're moving towards the kind of society where we aim to be more plural, and we are looking at a rhizomatic kind of structure, rather than a hierarchical kind of structure that always asks for a kind of efficiency. Time can be a constraint, but time can also be on our side. We need the time to evolve ourselves. And I keep seeing the arts community finding in many different ways to engage the government to talk about very important issues, like term licensing issues. There are many instances, however, like the IRCC where, from my perspective, I have always thought they are much more driven by the power-holders, because the IRCC sort of, you know, was really activated after the 9/11. And then there were a lot of organizations around the People's Association (PA), especially PA with the government, to bring them all together. Many things were discussed, but I really do not know if many of the difficult issues were actually brought to the general public. If the public are not able to speak, you know, about these issues, safely and fearlessly, then I think the idea of having a free space, the idea of having a democratic space, becomes questionable.

CCS: Maybe I'll just respond to the comment. Actually, the IRO predates the IRCC. The IRO is the Inter-Religious Organisation, the inter-faith organisation. They have existed way before we were independent. IRCC builds upon the work of the IRO because it builds on the trust of the IRO. And again we go back to the issue, does it mean that some of these issues, when we don't discuss publicly, that they're not discussed? I can accept that many of us would like to discuss such issues openly. But we can also discuss such issues behind closed doors, openly. The question is whether some of these things are broadcast, and if they are broadcast, whether it will change the dynamics of the discussion for some of these race and religious issues. Personally I would be rather cautious because — perhaps having gone through some of these discussions, they are very thorny issues. They are issues that one can easily take a different position, or take a different stance, if one is in a public space. When we say that we want to defend the common space, we will also necessarily mean that each of us give and take a bit. But for some of these difficult issues, it is very difficult for people to say, "I give some," and so forth — which is why we have open conversations away from the media glare, where people can share their views freely and openly. And it's not an ideological position whether it's just open or close; it's just a practical way of resolving the issues — allowing people the freedom and the space to discuss issues openly and privately without the media glare. So there will be some of these issues that we will continue to collaborate in quite a different fashion. For example, I will give you some more examples.

When it comes to defence, when it comes to reserves management, many of us would like to get involved in some of these things. But we also accept that some of these things just cannot be done in the way that is broadcast to everyone. But that doesn't stop us from having open and frank and hard conversations about what it is. It is just a question of how do we do it in a way that will bring about the solution for the betterment of our country.

For the arts community, it's not just about collaborating within the arts community. We all know that for a simple issue, what is allowed and what is not allowed, has great diversity of views beyond the arts community even. And whenever we make such a decision, it is taking into account the considerations of the arts community, which we must, and also at the same time, the larger community out there. So it is not so straightforward, but also at the same time, we welcome the participation and even the help of the arts community to even go out, explain to the public why this position is allowed, or not allowed, or why we take a certain position. That would be very powerful. That is really collective ownership, and collective respon-sibility, right? So, that is where I think we'd need to go forward, and I hope to enlist what I call the wisdom, the power, and the action, of our people in this. But collective ownership, and collective responsibility, is key to all this.

Chairperson: Let's get another question from the floor. The lady please, at the mic, go ahead.

Q3: Angie Chew, Brahm Center. Good morning, Minister. On the point of collaborative governance, to be effective, I think people need a certain amount of information and data. A sense of transparency has to come across to building that trust in civil societies. We don't have even data on how many households are considered below the poverty line. The poverty line has never been defined in Singapore. It's really hard to gauge how many people are left behind in the community and what we need to do collectively to help people rise up. How many people on welfare? We have no idea. So if that could be something that the government could be more transparent about, it would be helpful in many areas.

Chairperson: Okay, so basically you want more information and transparency on these kinds of issues so we can discuss them. Minister, please.

Q3: The second point I have is on nation-building, which is based on the past and building for the future. And why people are looking to perhaps even emigrate, I think there's something to do with feeling rooted in Singapore. And this point I'm raising is not new. At the end of the day we need to feel that there are places in Singapore that we can identify with, that we can be nostalgic about, and I think that many people would agree that bringing down the old National Library was probably a mistake, apart from Chinatown being so modernised that, when you walk in Chinatown, there is no soul. And so that comes to the latest matter on Mr Lee Kuan Yew's house. Basically that is a building of huge historic significance, and I would say that many people would like to see this house preserved, because where is going to be the history of Singapore being rooted to, more than any place than his residence? So I would therefore ask if the current leaders of PAP have the courage, to preserve this house and not be intimidated by one man's wish?

Chairperson: Okay, Minister, would you like to respond to those three points?

CCS: First, let me respond to the issues of the data. In fact actually, as we go forward to build the Smart Nation as we call it, there will be more data that we'd be sharing with everyone, and we hope that through this data, it can help us make better decisions for the siting of our social service officers, to the design of our transport system, and so forth. So yes, on the one hand, we will see more data being shared. On the other hand, I think we would also ask that whatever data that is being shared is handled with care, handled appropriately, so that it doesn't betray the trust of those people who shared the data. But definitely, you would see more data being shared. That's the first point.

The second thing is, it's not just about data being shared that is important. It's how we make best use of the data to design policies, to design systems that will help uplift the lives and livelihoods of our people. I know this conversation about the poverty line. I know many people would like us to have one definition of that. I personally have examined this issue for a long time in my previous capacity as the Minister for Social Affairs, and even as a young economics student. I don't think the world is defined so neatly, and can be categorised so neatly, as by one line. We have in our society, a continuum of people who need different types of help. To define a single line is convenient, but it may not be the most effective. I ask myself, if by defining that one line, does it help me to reach out to all the people in that continuum? Even if that one line is necessary, is that sufficient? And this is the reason why we have designed our system, not by the one line, but if you like, many lines, where different people across the spectrum with different needs are attended to appropriately. Can we do more, can we do better? Yes, definitely we can. And we will endeavour to do that.

You are also right that economic success and material wealth cannot define our national identity. In every of my conversation with the students in the institutes of higher learning, I always ask them this very simple question: "Why do you want to be a Singaporean?" Many of them will give me very good reasons about their family being here, job security, physical security, so on and so forth. And I will always challenge them — that if tomorrow, we have the proverbial, seven years of drought, seven years of recession, will you still stay here? Will you stay here like the 1965 generation that said that in spite of, I will rebuild this country for a better future for my people, if we have arrived at that stage… in spite of… then I think we have reached the point of "we" as a nation. But I am realistic. We aspire towards there, we may not be there yet. The best answer to my question of why you want to be a Singaporean — all those students give me all kinds of reasons — the best answer I've ever gotten from a student (from an Institute of Technical Education (ITE)), was simply this: "Minister, I don't know why you ask such a stupid question. I am a Singaporean. Full stop." There are not ifs and buts. There's no conditionality attached. Not because this country can give me what I want, not because this country can secure me a job and so on and so forth. This is where I belong. That even if this place goes back to 1965 and we have to re-build this country, I would stay here and re-build this country. If we can reach there, if the majority of our people can reach there, I think we can proudly say that we can survive for not just another 50 years, but perhaps another 500, a thousand years. That is the spirit of what makes us Singapore.

Yes we all miss many of the landmarks that have given way to development. Each and every landmark that we lose, we ask ourselves, whether we can find a better balance to preserving history and allowing the next generation to have more opportunities. Take my constituency as an example, and I share this with the students who receive the Edusave awards this year, I ask them, do any of them know what Holland Village, Holland Plains, Buona Vista used to be before what they are now? What has that to do with the cemetery, the Chinese cemetery behind the SPC petrol station, where it is the only cemetery in Singapore where the tombstones are neatly laid out in rows, because that used to be the cemetery of the clan. The clan, just as the clan in Bishan, Kwong Wai Siew, gave up their memories, gave up what they cherished in order for our generation to build our dreams upon them. Yes, each and every generation, we cherish our dreams, but each and every generation, we have to ask ourselves, to what extent and how prepared we are to allow our next generation to similarly build their dreams? There are no easy answers. If this generation, each and every one of us, hold dear to what we cherish, and not allow space for the next generation to grow and develop their dreams, then I am also not very sure how far we will go as a nation. So it is a fine balance. We hope to achieve both, conservation of our history, our memories, our legacies, and yet at the same time, create space for the next generation to grow.

Yes, the old National Library provided me with fond memories. That was the place I used to borrow my books. The red-brick building. That was the place that inspired me to want to be a librarian. Because that was the only place that I could borrow books, read books, free of charge, in an air-con environment, which was a luxury at that point in time.

Chairperson: Sir you are quite far down the road from being a librarian. I have to hurry you along, to ask you about the house, what's your view of that?

CCS: So I didn't become a librarian, I may still one day become a librarian, never too early to say. But let me round off with a comment and perhaps a response and remark. I have known Mr Lee for some time. I was in his… I was a fellow member of his GRC, and prior to that I have had the privilege to have some conversations with him, to work with him, and to see him in action. Not as much as perhaps many others, but in my limited interactions with him, he has impressed upon me a few things. One, his unceasing focus on the future of Singapore and Singaporeans. Even when he was very weak, whenever we met him, his first questions would always be, "Are the residents taken care of?" And the next few questions would inevitably be something along the lines of what are the forces impacting Singapore, and how is the current generation of leaders grappling with those challenges? This unceasing focus on the future of Singapore. Because I think he has committed his entire life to building a nation defying the odds of history, and the thing that made us… that was most poignant in my mind. [There] was one particular Tanjong Pagar grassroots event. He was very weak. He insisted on coming, to deliver a speech. When we sent him off that night to his car, all of us, the grassroots leaders, looked around. And instinctively we can kind of feel that kind of unspoken understanding, which is, he's so old, can we not do more to not let him worry on the future of Singapore and Singaporeans? So this is the one thing that he has taught me.

The second thing, I think whether the house or not the house, whether it's preserved or not preserved, I'm quite sure there is a diversity of views across Singapore. And even if you take a poll among the audience here, I'm quite sure you might not get a uniform answer. Because the question is: What is the best way to honour Mr Lee Kuan Yew? Is it to keep the house? Or is it to leave the spirit and the dream that he stood for? You will find your own answers, I have mine. My answer is that I hope that beyond the house, more important than the house, this generation and the rest will continue to uphold the very values that he has guided us in building this nation to defy the odds. That the best way to honour him is to continue to make sure that Singapore continues to succeed and thrive for generations to come. That future generations of Singaporeans, our children, our grandchildren, have the chance, and the desire, to be one, to be called Singaporeans. That Singapore will not go down in the history of the world as an interesting footnote. That if we look at the history of Southeast Asia where the borders have changed more frequently than compared to the equivalent period of the warring states in China, that we will not become an interesting footnote.

That to round it off, if I go back to the initial story that I started with, that for the many investors looking out there, that to the many of watchers of Singapore out there, that we give them every good reason possible for them to continue to support our continued success. If we can do that, then I think we are well on the way to building the nation. A nation that will survive in spite of. In spite of our resource limitations, in spite of our demographic challenges, so on and so forth. Then maybe one day, if we reach there, even as we pass on the baton to the next generation, we can say that we have been good stewards for our people and our country.

Chairperson: Okay, I think that's a good point with which to close our discussion. We've run overtime. Please join me in thanking the Minister and our panellists, and we can continue the discussion over coffee break. Thank you.

Cohesive Diversity?

Chairperson:
Walter Fernandez, Editor-in-Chief, MediaCorp Pte Ltd

Speaker:
Ng Chee Meng (NCM), then Acting Minister for Education (Schools)

Panel:
David Chan (DC), Lee Kuan Yew Fellow, Director of Behavioural Sciences Institute, Singapore Management University

Elaine Ho (EH), Department of Geography, Faculty of Arts and Social Sciences, National University of Singapore

Hassan Ahmad (HA), Technical Adviser & Executive Director, Corporate Citizen Foundation

Chairperson: The topic for our second session is "cohesive diversity". This really builds on the discussion in the first panel, where we talked about good politics as Warren described it. Now, Singapore has evolved significantly. Our traditional divides of race, religion, language — these have changed significantly in the last years. Now, Singapore society is looking at inequality of wealth distribution; the influx of foreigners; the divide between the young and old; inter-marriages; issues surrounding LGBT rights; whether a children's book about two male penguins raising a baby chick is suitable reading material for our young; whether counting down to the new year, being entertained by Adam Lambert is suitable, and whether junior colleges should be named Eunoia or Ee-you-know-ya. These faultlines really challenge the cohesiveness and tolerance and open space that our society has enjoyed over the last 50 years. Will the diversity lead to greater division, or will we eke out the strengths that diversity brings with it. We need to explore the Singapore model on how to deal with this and overcome the challenges posed by diversity.

I have with me a distinguished panel. Let me start by introducing the speaker for today, Mr Ng Chee Meng. He's the Acting Minister for Education and concurrently Senior Minister of State for Transport, and before joining Cabinet, he was Singapore's Chief of Defence Force. To my left, I have Professor David Chan, Lee Kuan Yew Fellow, and Director of the Behavioural Sciences Institute at the Singapore Management University; Associate Professor Elaine Ho, who is from the Geography Department at the National University of Singapore, and Mr Hassan Ahmad, who is Executive Director of the Corporate Citizen Foundation. This is a private sector alliance, targeted at regional humanitarian missions. I welcome the panel and our speaker, and could we have a round of applause for them. I will now hand over to Chee Meng for his opening remarks.

NCM: Professor Wang Gungwu, Chairman of the Governing Board of the Lee Kuan Yew School of Public Policy; Professor Tommy Koh, Special Advisor to IPS; Janadas, Director of the Institute of Policy Studies, my friends, distinguished guests, ladies and gentlemen, a very good morning to all of you. I am very delighted to be here this morning to share my thoughts with you, and more importantly, to hear your perspective as one Singapore. The term "cohesive diversity", according to Mr Ho Kwon Ping, is a delightful oxymoron. And indeed, it is so. But this morning, I shan't go too much into the English of it. Diversity in itself is actually a neutral concept. It simply means variety. Therefore, the merits or pitfalls of diversity are context-specific. For example, in an organisation, diversity can be a source of strength, because from this diversity, different ideas, different viewpoints can be put on the table, and the resultant decision would most likely benefit from this plethora of viewpoints for the marketplace. However, this is assuming that after the decision is made, all would rally behind the decision. By the very same example, what if even after a decision is taken, different parties don't quite buy in, and continue to pull in different directions? Then the very same diversity divides. Therefore, whether diversity brings strength or diversity divides, depends not only in the thinking, but also in the doing.

As such, harnessing diversity for strength involves both ideation and also unity of action. Likewise, for Singapore, there is more than one social, cultural or economic group, including racial and religious groups. Diversity can either be a good thing, or a bad thing. In our history, as some of you older gentlemen and ladies have lived through, we have had to manage significant tensions where diversity led to social unrest. In our earlier years, Singapore faced racial riots — intra-racial riots, ideological differences that threaten to pull our society apart. But over the last 50 years, we have rallied together and forged what I can probably call cohesive diversity in Singapore today.

Singapore's cohesive diversity actually started out as a vision, an ideation, crystalised on our pledge. In our earlier years, the pledge emerged as we struggled to forge a sense of national identity, a sense of nationhood. We pledge ourselves first, as a united people, committed to build a nation regardless of race, language or religion. Our founding fathers believed that race, language and religion had the potential to divide. The late Mr Rajaratnam wrote the pledge to call upon Singaporeans to be united and overcome these differences or diversities, as we build a common future together as one united people. So, getting the vision right is very important.

But the vision alone would not have led us to where we are today, as one Singapore. So what did? In my view, it is largely due to our inclusive politics and politics that drove us towards this vision. These are careful policies, deliberate policies, practical, pragmatic policies. Our politics did not shy away from difficult decisions to create common spaces, for all groups to live, work and play together. Common spaces that we should continue to guard jealously. These policies create, enlarge, and defend our common spaces, and they are not static. These policies will evolve over time, even as our society evolves and matures.

Today, more of us are championing causes we believe in. Causes such as environmental sustainability, animal rights, and so forth. As we globalise, income inequality would remain an issue. Singaporeans ourselves are also becoming more diverse, due to more inter-racial marriages and maybe even immigration. The texture of our society has become more complex, and the idea of multiculturalism has become more nuanced. We want Singaporeans to care about our community, and to serve. And we want Singaporeans who choose to believe in Singapore, and who believe in making a difference here.

The challenge is: Will we be able to continue to progress towards our vision of one united people, even as we appear to be more different and diverse? Our vision has not changed, as I spoken to many Singaporeans. But even as we disagree on issues, we agree on one thing. Our common vision, as in our pledge, one united people. What will make a real difference is how we continue with our inclusive politics and policies. These policies, as I have said, may change over time, but the core elements such as education, meritocracy, and leaving no Singaporean behind, must remain. As a society, Singaporeans must respect all differences, and proactively defend our common spaces, regardless of whether we are Singapore born, or new citizens. Regardless of religion, and regardless of whether we are rich or poor. Our integration and naturalisation champions actively reach out to the new citizens and Permanent Residents (PRs). And over time, these new citizens and PRs can contribute more to our community, and at the same time, expand their social network. And I'm quite glad to see that we are on the right track. Back when I was in the Singapore Armed Forces (SAF), as we set up the SAF Volunteer Corps, we attracted a lot of interest. I recall a particular gentleman, a Singaporean PR, who wanted to sign up as a volunteer. Why? Because he gets a little... I quote, he gets "a little jealous" of the common bond that Singaporean males share, as national servicemen. So even as we welcome new PRs or new citizens in this diverse city, we are already creating bonds.

On the way forward, we will continue to refine our Singapore approach to diversity. It is not just going to be through government policies, but I think it will be through inclusive politics, as I said earlier. Every Singaporean will have a part to play. Our community will have a part to play. And in the true spirit of drawing strength from diversity, I would very much like to hear your views later. I hope it won't be a monologue where I answer your questions only. And really, conversations about diversities, we all know, can be emotionally charged — especially among those who view it as a zero-sum game. How can we have these conversations in an informed and constructive manner where viewpoints, whether you are in the majority or in the minority, are respected and probably considered? In some sensitive areas, there may be no definitive consensus today, even as we recognise that the new equilibrium may be needed in the future. What do we as a society need to do in that process of evolution and transition? How can we be more resilient as one united people, harness the strength from our diversity, and never allow it to pull us apart? How can we galvanise individuals, including all of you, all of us here, in this room today, in our call to action to help society find balance amidst the diversity of views, amidst a rapidly changing world. I look forward to hearing your views, thank you very much.

Chairperson: Thank you, Minister. Now I would like to invite the panel, to make a few comments, and also to ask questions that they might have, of Minister. We will start with David.

DC: Thanks, Minister and Chairman. I think most of us can agree on the good things — diversity is both a strength and weakness, depending on how you do it. We need to be united and so on. I think the challenge for a conference like this, and also for the public discourse, is how to do it. I think what should be done is relatively clear. If we do a survey, probably at least 9 out of 10 — at least nine meaning it's over 90% — will actually agree with some of the basic principles on what is good. I think the "how" is the difficult part.

I think there is some hope, not just because of the vote in the General Elections (GE). But I think there's a more informed public discussion, and more people are more able and willing to speak up on how to do certain things. The challenge is for both the leadership and the various stakeholders to understand what we mean by the positives and negatives of diversity. The negatives can actually be explosive. As we can see, many of the sectoral fights, terrorism, actually come from failure to appreciate how different social identities can co-exist. I think we need to be quite aware of the negatives, as we pursue the positives. At the same time, the positives are aspirational, and if we don't pursue them, I think we will just become isolated pockets, staying within Singapore, and that's not going to be very helpful, when something negative really happens.

With that brief comment, I thought I just want to first agree with the Minister, that when a decision is made, we got to kind of live with it, and rally behind the decision. I just like to add, though, that the decision needs to be adaptive. After the decision has been made, we must be able, and ensure that processes allow the recognition that the decision needs to change after a while. And when that happens, the trick is for the leadership to ensure that, well, it is not necessarily a U-turn, but how we need to now make the decision a little bit differently. I think that kind of dynamism, that kind of leadership and trust is very important.

The second point, I think about how a decision has been made, that we need to rally behind, is not to forget the decision-making process. One of the reasons that people don't rally behind the decision, is usually not the decision itself, but the process in which the decision is arrived. And then — those of us who know about outcome fairness — the process fairness is another. So focusing on the fairness of the process, I think it becomes practical. And within that context, I would also argue that the pledge is very important; I recite it, you recite it, but we are Singaporeans. If you throw a ball when you get out of this room, and it falls on somebody's head… actually the chances of it falling on a Singaporean is six out of 10, because four out of 10 are non-citizens. And with that in mind, I don't think it is quite possible to use our national pledge to speak to the four out of 10, because they are not citizens. So I think we need to be a bit careful that while Singaporeans can adhere to the pledge, the national anthem, the way we are brought up, [we need to] recognise that the four out of 10 may need a different approach. And that means we need to think through what are some of the unifying concepts to address diversity — at least for the 4 out of 10, if not 10 out of 10.

And I would suggest that we think about the concept of home. Minister spoke about the PR wanting to do military [service]. Quite an extreme example, but I am sure there are also other examples. And I would argue that if you look at that positively, it's because the PR thought this is a good home away from home. This is a good second home. So whether you are a single — then you won't have the idea that we talked about this morning, that I want my children to do better, because you are single, you don't have children — and there're quite a number of singles around, so whether you are single, you are married, you are citizens, you are PR, or you are non-citizens, I think the idea that Singapore can be your home within a community, can be a unifying concept. So you can think about here as "home away from home", a good home, and for Singapore, this is your home. And when you are away, you will think about coming back home. I think the idea of home within a community is something that we need to think through a little bit more, and give it a little bit more weightage, and when the community thinks that it's the context in which you have your home, the idea that you will speak up, the idea that you will just not talk but take action, becomes real. So, this is one of several ideas that we can, several ways that we can make ideas into action. Thank you.

Chairperson: Thanks David. Minister, would you like to take up any of those points, about adaptive decisions, the decision making process being fair, and using more than the pledge.

NCM: Well, humans have different levels of identities. So, in many ways, I agree with what David has said. Our pledge appeals to Singaporeans, because it starts with the premise, "We, the citizens of Singapore," it appeals to the 60, 70% of us, in this geographical location, called the state of Singapore. So, in that, using the pledge to rally 70% of our people, it's not a trivial one. While, if you can recall, the national day celebrations, we do have Kit Chan singing, *Home*.

In parallel, we can appeal to different levels of identification, as individual, as a father, I would have a different identity. The Ng clan has a certain identity of heritage, as a community we have different identities. So I don't look at it as a zero-sum appeal towards rallying a sense of home or Singapore heartbeat. It is through different policies, different hands, different initiatives that, over longer periods of time, that forged identities. But at the end of it all, when we discuss Singapore perspectives, what is the prevalent and dominant identity we want to cultivate? I would submit to all of us, that it will be a Singapore shared identity, a national identity. Because for the next 50 years, there will be many, many challenges that will abound, some we can see in the short term. There will be many challenges that are beyond the horizon at the moment. How do we have the fabric that will hold us together, with common ideals, a common vision, that not just appeals to the intellect, but appeals to all the different levels of the make up of the human being. So I agree with what you have said in many, many ways, but I would like to expand the space in which we discuss cohesive diversity. Because if we narrow it too much, ironically, there's no diversity or possibility.

Chairperson: Thank you, Minister. Elaine?

EH: Thank you, Walter and Minister. So, I want to talk a bit about the idea of "we", and also building on David's metaphor of home, which as a geographer, I appreciate very much. I think when we talk about "we" in this age of globalisation, especially in the case of Singapore as a global city state, it may not be sufficient to only think about it in terms of citizenship status. So, we have… I think citizenship is about a process. And for people who are born in Singapore, and grew up in Singapore, perhaps it is more natural to identify as a citizen. But in that process of identifying as a citizen ourselves, we also create "othering" kind of categories. So, for example, Singaporean-born citizens may not be so welcoming towards new citizens. And even towards PRs. And I think in some of our policies we are starting to see a sharpening divide between foreigners, citizens and PRs. So my worry is that these types of categorisations actually could impede the integration of new citizens and PRs.

And I think I also want to bring up the CMIO model — Chinese, Malay, Indian, Others, that have been the typical approach in which we approach governance and policymaking in Singapore. So, the CMIO model filters into housing, into education, and more. However, I question if this model is still capacious enough to accommodate the greater diversity in Singapore today. So we see the Others category expanding at an accelerated rate, and then, at the same time, the irony is that within the Chinese and the Indian categories, we see the growing differentiations with new migrants coming from China and from South Asia. So I wonder if the CMIO model is actually still a good way for us to think about managing ethnicity and the intersecting types of identities that different kinds of people converging in Singapore today may have.

Chairperson: Elaine, I will just challenge you on that. Do you have an alternative to a CMIO model?

EH: In terms of the CMIO model? Well personally, I think that the CMIO model has served its purpose. I mean, it's probably been about 50 years now, and I would actually like to see these categorisations dissolved, more so. I realise we do have mixed race categories now, but that is another form of categorisation.

Chairperson: Okay, Minister. Dissolve the CMIO model.

NCM: Thank you Elaine. Well, again it comes back to how human beings actually identify ourselves. From the earliest seeds of civilisation where we belong to a small group of hunter-gatherers, to civilisation today. Humans do not exist just as individuals — even as we exist as individuals, we find solace in groups, in clans, develop into villages, develop into kingdoms, industrial age/revolution that redefined human organisation, human governance, and to today, where the information technology revolution is outpacing governance, the models of governance. When you look back in this long history of human civilisation, well, we got to ask ourselves: Will we be in our ideation, even as we desire to nuance the differences of C, M, I, O, will it be possible and practicable? This idea actually Kwon Ping spoke about in the series of lectures he had — and after a while, with his own conversations with his friends that are minorities, actually, he said that, what he said probably wasn't the most circumspect. Because when we talk to our friends who are in the minority, if you were to remove this, how will it impinge on their rights when we want to blur it [ethnic lines] as a majority race in Singapore? But if we were to blur it, who will represent their interests? How would we design inclusive politics to make sure that my Malay brethren will be represented in Parliament? How will we create policies that will ensure that my Indian brethren will be represented in Parliament? So while there are ideals of expanding or doing away with this, I think we need to match it with the realities of life as we see it. Between the ideals and the practicalities of politics, how do we find the path forward? So I would be very, very careful to move away from principles that have served us very well for so long. Is there space for evolution? I fully agree with you that we should continue to think about this space for evolution. So if I am not mistaken, before I have joined government, our government had also explored giving parents the choice to put their children in whatever category of race, when the child is born. Is it a big dramatic step? Well, arguably no. But is it the evolution of looking at CMIO in a different light? I would say yes. So some of these things I think would involve some evolution, and you must give it time.

Chairperson: Elaine, is that enough for you? Being able to label your children Chinese, Indian....

EH: Sorry, I can't really hear you.

Chairperson: Is that answer sufficient? Are you happy just being able to label your children Chinese, Indian....

EH: Well, if I may follow up in that case, since you've asked, we talk about minority representation, but with the changing demographics in Singapore, we have an increasing number of minorities. And I think that while we may privilege certain types of identities that are tied to being the so-called... maybe we can say the pioneer ethnic categories, the Chinese, Malay, Indian, Others. So these are the ethnic categories that emerge from the time when Singapore became independent till today. But now with a growing range of minority populations, how do we then also represent these other kinds of ethnic groups that are congregating in Singapore today?

Chairperson: That is quite a specific question, Minister.

NCM: Oh, in our system, civic society conversations like these, in our own political system, in the Group Representation Constituency (GRC) system, it's all designed to have minorities incorporated, so that there will always be voices other than the majority in government. But looking even beyond this specific design of our GRC system, if you could recall, Mr Lee Kuan Yew's words: This will not a Chinese nation, this will not be an Indian nation, this will not be a Malay nation. We are all in it together. I think under that umbrella of a principled approach to inclusive politics, is where we find the space. And, as I said, it is a long journey ahead for the next 50 years, for us to consider. And within this principle, where can we find the nuanced policies to allow evolution, to allow space, for these discussions to find a new alternative level. I think that will probably be the better approach towards such sensitive areas.

Chairperson: Thank you minister. Hassan, jump in.

HA: Thank you, Walter.

NCM: May I just interrupt for a minute? This is really not the best way to have a conversation. Maybe I should just stand up, so that in the spirit of cohesive diversity, really engage in conversation. I can't even see you when you talk, and I hear all kinds of echoes down here.

HA: So I think we have got decent politics and sound policies all these years that have allowed for our harmonious co-existence, which includes inter-racial and inter-religious relations. And this is in line with the spirit of what our founding prime minister said. Everyone shall have a place in this country. The Singapore model has worked really well. The global religious diversity report[1] ranked Singapore as the most diverse, in terms of religions, out of 232 countries. And PM Lee said that this was an unusual, unnatural state of affairs.

So, we know that the Singapore model has worked tremendously well. But we are also under no delusions that Singapore is vulnerable; it remains vulnerable in terms of the things that are happening around us. Of course, there are no guarantees of harmony, sustained harmony amongst us. What more should we do now, especially given that there is increasing religiosity, increasing migration. This will also increase the challenge, or the challenges of inter-faith, as well as intra-faith. So how do we engage the different strata of society? I think everyone needs to be educated. We can't take things for granted, everybody knows we can't be complacent.

Interestingly, the schools have started social studies as a compulsory [subject], together with the humanities. Back in the 1980s, when I was in secondary school, we had to do religious knowledge. From the Education Ministry, are we ready to inject inter-religious knowledge into the syllabus or curriculum, for the 'O' and 'A' Levels? And also, from the military, are we also ready to also inject inter-religious knowledge as part of the curriculum for our National Service (NS) men, reservist, and also the active units, Minister?

---

[1] See the Religious Diversity Index from the Pew Research Centre, http://www. pewforum.org/2014/04/04/global-religious-diversity/.

NCM: I would not go into a content-specific answer, because this is really not a forum for policymaking. But maybe, when you ask those questions, while I said that the pledge rallies, we didn't quite explore why did we succeed. Why did inclusive politics succeed? I think over the last 50 years, as I said, once certain personalities have put forth a certain ideal for us to go through, Singapore rallied together as one people, within the space. There were a lot of agreements and disagreements. But over 50 years, one of the invaluable things in our society is trust. Trust between the people and the government. Why would some community subjugate their interests for the wider group? Because they can see the validity of the vision, and they trust that in action, consistently over time, the government has the ability, the integrity and probably most importantly, the track record, over periods of time, over different crisis, different contingencies, they have tested, and we have come forth to hold on to those ideals, by our record. So...

(Someone brings him a chair) Oh, thank you. It's actually okay.

(To the audience) This is more a conversation, don't you think?

So, the specific issues about whether education can play a role, I definitely think so. But whether we should reintroduce inter-religious studies, inter-racial studies, and the plethora of diversities of issues, well, I think we can think about it. But under education, and then variegating our system out into the compulsory education design of Ministry of Education (MOE), we actually brought together disparate schools — in 1959, where we had Malay schools, Indian schools, Chinese schools that were pulling us apart. And we went into compulsory education — you have a common system for six years — it allows our children, of my time, me, to play, study, and sometimes fight, sometimes cry together, with my friends in the Malay community, in the Indian community, so on and so forth. So the six years that we have put into the system are known, but not widely appreciated, that we find a balance between forging a national identity for the first six years in primary schools, to allow Singaporeans with unique talents, with different levels of abilities to explore and chase the rainbows. So within this, even in the education system, you can see a delicate balance, between forging identity — which in some ways is uniformity — and allowing the strengths of diversity to come through, and allow Singapore society to function at some optimal levels. Will this balance change over the next 50 years? Probably so. But it will be contextualised to that generation, to see how you would find that equilibrium that will suit Singapore and Singaporeans best, at that time.

Does that answer your question?

(Chairperson stands) Now, I don't know whether to stand or sit.

So structure makes a difference to have meaningful conversations.

QUESTION AND ANSWER SESSION

Chairperson: To have meaningful conversations, I'm going to stand. I think in the first panel, we didn't get as much from the audience as we would like to. I am going to throw it open to the floor now. I see a hand raised, straightaway. Could someone get a mic out here?

Q1: Minister, Singapore is a predominantly Chinese country. It will continue to be a predominantly Chinese country. This morning we have heard about collaborative government, and you spoke about inclusiveness and diversity. And I think we have arrived where we are because of very extraordinary measures — legislative and political — which defy any definition you see outside in the world such that we do not suffer from the tyranny of majoritarianism. We may suffer from it in the future if we are not careful, which means we have to make more extraordinary measures in the future, so the minorities do not just have a proportion of influence which is small, but I think continue to enjoy a special place in Singapore. So, as a member of the future leadership, I would like to know what are the extraordinary things that you think we should continue to do, so that you don't end up collaborators very comfortable on their own, and compromise the interest of the minority who have all along been part and parcel of a larger Chinese Singapore community.

NCM: Well that's a very good question. I think, in this, the structures are somewhat designed, and serving us reasonably well. The processes would really be the focal point in the way forward. How do we ensure that Zainal Sapari, my colleague in my GRC, comes together with us to discuss things?

In the process, how do we actually formulate the way forward together? Not so much as making extraordinary concessions or extraordinary treatments, but as one entity, as a polity, how do we engage in the process? And what the President has also said, as the last point, engaging Singaporeans, and together, owning the very policies that we design for the future. I think that is probably the method forward. Specifically, were certain issues to surface, then I think, having different representation to articulate our viewpoints, will be very, very important. Not so much the structures — that I think have served us quite well — but in the process, in this period of time.

Chairperson: Other questions, yes. Okay, we have a missing mic again.

Q2: [My] name is Suee Chieh from NTUC Enterprise. I was encouraged by the previous question, because my question has the same context, but a slightly different take. Firstly, Janadas this morning explained very clearly the importance of perpetuating our shared identity, which means deepening our shared context as Singaporeans, as a citizenry. But of course we are competing against other shared identities. Be it being a Muslim, you see a tremendous rise in militancy throughout the world, be it Christian conservatism, liberalism, or Indian nationalism if India emerges in the next 50 years. So that is the background in which the new leadership has to take Singapore. So my argument is not just about process, right? It is about how Singapore, because [it has been] so extraordinary in the first 50 years... it was a remarkable reflection of an extraordinary leadership. So what kind of leaders do we need, coming to the next 10 years, 20 years, 30 years? Is it the kind of leadership you see in Mr Lee Kuan Yew? Or is it a more consultative, inclusive leadership of Goh Chok Tong? Do we need good economies, or do we need good union leaders? What kind of leadership do we need? So I want to hear your response to it. What kind of personalities do we need? Because I think that is quite an important question.

Chairperson: Yup, thank you.

NCM: Good question. It is not in my view, the most complete question, because, in Mr Lee's era, cohesive diversity was not real. The tensions in society were pulling us apart. So what kind of leadership do we need in that period? Consultative? Would that have worked as well? I don't know, because we can't wind back the clock. We can only have an intellectual argument. But as we succeeded together as a country, Singaporeans became better educated, with good viewpoints, with good ideas. How then do we evolve our leadership style, as a government? Then I think, Mr Goh's era, when it became more consultative, was the best way forward. The next 50 years, I think, personally, this dimension of consultative leadership, co-ownership of our outcomes, will be even more important. So in each era, we don't just put a form of, style of leadership, into a specific vacuum. We need to understand what is the context, and therefore find the best way forward. And I think it is quite common in Singapore, for all Singaporeans to know what Mr Lee Kuan Yew has done for us. We appreciate what he has done, but many of us, in ideas today, would want our voices to be heard, so that we can participate. And at this stage of our country's evolution, well, I am glad that we have almost [a] thousand five [hundred] people here? That we can collectively speak in a rational manner, without charged emotions, to find out who thinks what, how can we think better, and then ultimately, how do we design policies that will move us collectively forward — coming back to the pledge, as one united people, and within that space, under-standing and having the humility to know that my view may not be the primary way. It is one of a plethora of views, and after long or short consultation, depending on context again, what decision is taken, and whether that overarching identity to move ourselves forward as Singapore, in the sense of sometimes subjugating your view beneath someone else's. So in the conversations that we have, it is not about winning the argument. I personally, very much want to hear the best argument, and then formulate my position. Not the other way round. I don't come here with a position to push. I come here, in a nice environment like this, with the luxury of time, to hear and find the best position. But if I were to go back into my previous profession as the Chief of Defence Force, in crisis, I may not have the luxury of time. And therefore we do all the preparatory work, all the exercises, to think through as many things as possible, but when it is time to call for action, without the luxury of time, then, let's do it together, respect the decision, and go forth. We have this range of possibilities.

Chairperson: In the interest of keeping this a conversation, I will put the same question to David as well, the type of leadership you expect to see. [That's] the question asked from the floor.

DC: Well I expect to see… maybe I will say what kind of leadership I want. "Expect to see" is quite a different question from the leadership I want. I think the leadership I want and I hope you want and I am sure the Minister wants too, is one that is principled and adaptive. I don't include the word "pragmatic" because it is arguable whether pragmatic is a principle, and if you include it, it becomes "PAP" (principled, adaptive and pragmatic). Principled is enough to include pragmatism as one of the principles. I think the important thing is that this is translated into individuals; the people on the ground (walking on the street, watching television) don't use words like "pragmatism" and "principled". They look at who you are, which means they use words like, "Are you competent [and] do you have character?" Competence and character are the two main things that leaders must never give up. Of course we can debate what is character and what is competence, [whether] it is actual or perceived, but those are fundamentals.

Please let me say something about the CMIO model. I just want to remind ourselves that we all have social identities. For instance, I am Singaporean, I am Chinese, I am male and so on. Our social identities get activated and I cannot change my race. I would suggest all to be careful when we talk about the CMIO model because there are some things (aspects to identity) that are fundamental, that you are born with and cannot change; it comes with a certain context. We did not choose to be of a particular sex or race and so on and it becomes important that such ascribed status that we are born with must not have a policy whereby [these people] end up advantaged or disadvantaged. If you don't want to talk about male and female, there will be no Women's Charter. Similarly, if you do not want to talk about the CMIO model, then we need to ask what kind of policies have to be erased. When that happens, is it good or bad? That kind of thinking is important. We separate that from the CMIO model. Is it impeding national identity? I don't think so. All the national surveys show that I can be very Malay and very Singaporean at the same time. These [surveys] are anonymous so people are not trying to be socially desirable. Bear in mind, when we say do away with CMIO, what are we doing away with? I am not saying that everything is fine but be careful about what we are doing away with.

NCM: If I could just take that point a little further, in my younger days many of us identified ourselves first as Chinese Singaporeans, Malay Singaporeans or Indian Singaporeans. Today when I interact with folks on the ground, almost unanimously, [people say that] "I am a Singaporean Chinese, I am a Singaporean Indian, I am a Singaporean Malay." The CMIO model and the way that we have gone about it has actually — at two levels — at the highest level, forged the national identity because of the rallying call of the pledge. At the second-order level, we have continued to allow, encourage the propagation of our unique cultures and heritage, so that we draw strength from the diversity of our heritage. We are not quite like the Americans where we want to assimilate and produce Singaporeans who are non-Chinese, non-Malay and non-Indian but Singaporean, and this is a state policy that we want to have the cake and eat it too — to have the diversity of our heritage back to whichever ancestry, build those strengths and at the same time build a new sense of nationhood; and the CMIO model [largely] functioning at the second layer, whether in our education system or our housing policies have largely succeeded, with somewhat more of a retrospective credit perhaps, of rallying ourselves as a country, as a rallying call.

EH: I agree that the CMIO model has served us well, and it has enabled us to forge a strong national identity. But I also am concerned that the CMIO model has become sedimented to such an extent that it defines Singaporean identity narrowly in those categories, and it may not be able to sufficiently cope with the greater diversity, the proliferation of different ethnic groups and nationalities that are being represented in Singapore today.

And that's why I come back to the point that I started with, when we think about "we" as a category, we shouldn't just limit it to Singaporeans, because Singapore encompasses a greater range of people now. Some of them are temporary migrants, some of them are new PRs, some of them are potential citizens. When we think about "we" only in terms of citizens or Singaporeans, it excludes a large proportion of our population, as well as the complexity of the kind of identities that are being represented now. I am not saying that the CMIO model has not served us, and it continues to serve us, but are there ways of thinking about it in more nuanced ways.

NCM: I think there are, and it may not be the primacy of government policies then. It is in our communities. if I were to take myself off as a Minister, going back to the grassroots, how do I encourage our communities to welcome new citizens, new PRs and at the grassroots level, come together and build bonds? But these things take time, and many times cannot be dictated. It takes individuals like all of us in the room, individuals functioning in the community to make sure that the minorities, whether it is race or nationality, are not pushed out of our lives in Singapore. But, I must say that being a Singapore citizen must have unique privileges — there must be differentiation, otherwise it is very difficult to define what is the Singapore state and what are the privileges of being Singaporean as well. These are some of the things that I suppose have to balance out: Which category would require our closest attention, who do we encourage to become part of us, and who, that sometimes we just don't have the space to accommodate? Those are the realities of governance.

Q3: My question is regarding rights of minority groups like LGBT community and single mothers. We are often told when we are talking about issues that deal with these communities, that such issues are polarising and it is most practical and beneficial to wait for society to evolve before we can see any change being implemented in our policies. I have two observations: (1) it means that protection of such minorities' interests will only be granted when the majority approves, which defeats the purpose of protecting minorities, (2) sometimes the time and pace waiting for these changes to happen might not keep up with the needs that we need to deal with, for example, [having] LGBT in schools, housing needs, and healthcare needs. My question is, while we are waiting for society to evolve, should the government... is there a role for the government to intervene to take steps to protect minorities' interests in the meanwhile and to help change misconceptions of such minority communities?

NCM: There are policies that are already answering to these needs, whether single mothers, where Ministry of Social and Family Development (MSF) policies and Housing & Development Board (HDB) policies are answering to these needs. But for the other part of the question, you asked about LGBT issues, whether we can come together as a society. My basic answer to you again is the space for consensus-building in this [issue] is small, because the viewpoints are quite opposed. Very much like perhaps in the past, when we had racial riots, those viewpoints are far apart as well. Then, can we have the patience, to educate, to allow the processes of discussion, of forging common bonds to move this relationship forward. There are some things we can draw from history, slightly different context, but nevertheless with the same texture. In some things the best way forward is to allow it to evolve; society changes, each generation have our own outlook of life, own ideals, and whether over time we will find new equilibriums that society at large accepts. On those two parts, I would not quite put them in the same category — single mothers with needs for housing, with other needs for us to help with the children — all those are spaces that we have more convergence that we can design policies. In other areas, we have to allow the evolution of time so that society can find the new water level.

Q4: Minister, in the interest of further integrating the category of children who are likely to become leaders, can you rethink the Special Assistance Plan (SAP) schools system? The parent of a high-ability Malay girl told me that she was transferred out of the school when it became a SAP school. One of the young Indian MPs at the alumni giving a speech said that on his first day in law school he had coffee with two Chinese who said they have never before ever had a conversation with an Indian. They were having a [conversation] because he spoke Mandarin and he heard them call him a "dirty Indian". So he answered politely, of course he was upset they were having coffee together. If all these people had been in school together, it might better integrate the future leadership.

NCM: As I mentioned earlier, we only start SAP schools when our kids reach 14, and there are specific reasons why SAP schools are part of our history to promote deeper understanding of culture and heritage and so on and so forth. There are six years where our kids would intermingle, and in the variegated landscape of secondary schools, there will be some cases like you have mentioned, that may fall in between the policy designs. But by

53

and large, over 12 years, you will have different opportunities to interact, to understand, to grow up together. And if all else fails, if it is a boy, you still have National Service. I understand that the examples quoted, some of them do have fewer friends from the minority races but in the process the whole system, we allow many, many possibilities.

Q5: My question overlaps with the gentlemen just now, so I thought I would just add on some points. My question is: How are we to achieve cohesive identity when groups like the single mothers and the LGBT community are still marginalised — marginalised at the edge of society in the sense that they do not have the same rights and benefits, like childcare benefits or rights to reserve Build-to-Order (BTO) flats. For example, the petition to move Adam Lambert from the New Year's Countdown actually attracted 20,000 signatures. On the next day, there is a counter-petition, attracting a similar number of signatures. We can see here that we have two very different groups, with very different worldviews. On one hand, a group with pro-family values who believes in the nuclear family unit and the other with a more liberal view towards LGBT rights. My question is: Does the government have a definitive stand on LGBT rights, and how is it going to handle this delicate clash in values?

NCM: I have no new answer for you, as I have answered the gentlemen. Let society find its watermark. When you talk about two different groups, as I mentioned, to forge cohesive diversity, do we come into the conversation to force our viewpoint or do we come in with the humility and respect to also consider other viewpoints, and at the end of it, how do we look at the decision or the solution as the best way forward. After a conversation, especially in policymaking, we just cannot agree to disagree and walk away. It is not just a simple debate but when we have the luxury of time for evolution, maybe that is the solution. It will not be satisfactory especially for a bright young girl like you in a school, did you say NUS High?

Q5: National Junior College.

NCM: Okay, still very technical, science-based education. Well you want a cause-effect outcome almost immediately. But in the human dynamics of society and governance, sometimes time is a great resource. Don't have to rush it, let society evolve and take up their own civic conversation to find a new turn. As for the single mothers, I don't know if it is an issue of identity or pragmatic policies. I will recount a case to you. I met a single mother just yesterday at the Edusave Awards — I won't mention her name because this is too large an audience. She came up to thank me because we spent three months helping her find a roof over their heads. We can design the best policies, but there will always be marginal interfaces with different policies that people will fall through the cracks. Then how do we as a government, as a public service, come together to answer these unique cases that policy cannot cover? If we had more success stories of empathy where my colleagues in MSF are trying their best and doing a good job, we will be able to share more of these stories. I have this lady who is moving out of my immediate vicinity to another place. She had tears in her eyes yesterday, and asked whether she can come back to see us. I think we had made a difference. I don't know whether it is an entire difference across different segments of society, but each case we deal with it with empathy and with the attitude of service. I will finish the story. I asked this lady — I have another case of a lady who is going through a divorce with three kids. I asked this first lady, would you mind if I link you up so that you, now having benefitted from the work of the community, share your experience to provide support, counsel to work with this lady? This is what I mean by each one of us has a part to play. It is not between you and the government. It is us as a collective forging our way ahead to the next 50 years.

As we stand on SG51, I emphasise the pledge because there will be many thorny issues that we may not have consensus on that we have to find a way forward, and under this umbrella, where is the space for us to disagree where society still has the fabric to hold itself together? Or will your generation let all the disagreements pull us apart. That will be your role. Okay?

Q6: I have a question, a suggestion and an observation. One of the questions that I have, as spoken very clearly by Mr Janadas, is about our pledge. It is a 1965, 1966 kind of finalisation. Gender is not there. Race, religion, language. It is a primary issue when we want to talk about diversity, because in our Constitution too, gender is not there. I would like to hear, that's my question, the views of yourself, Minister, when can gender come in, both into the pledge and into the Constitution. The suggestion that I have is: It is my hope that we will take more seriously the CMIO model. I like what Professor David Chan has said — we have got to examine it. But I am also with Professor Elaine Ho — is this an outmoded model, not that it is totally all wrong, but how do we need to modify it in a changing society? On top of that it is quite divisive — we are thinking it brings a lot of equality but sometimes I think it is quite divisive. The third point that I would like to talk about is the Third Convention on the Elimination of All Forms of Racial Discrimination. Singapore has signed it and it is about to be ratified. If we go through the clauses very clearly, equality is mentioned across many spectrums, including foreigners. I think there needs to be a more serious engagement on this issue and I like that the topic has got cohesive diversity with a question mark because it is an oxymoron. So how are we going to engage in this is very important.

This is for all of us. I think we are as a citizenry over-relying on the political leaders to give us all our answers. We need to find a number of the solutions.

NCM: I agree, especially with your last point about political leaders giving all the answers. In my preamble I said I would like to hear the views of the rest of us. Because it is not my purview to change the pledge — it is *our* purview. Do we want to do it? Or does it have enough space that we already assume gender equality in our treatment of our citizens. I don't have the answer, in fact I will never have the answer for you. Thankfully you put the last point across that you are looking too much at me for answers, so it gives me a way out. I am here, like I said, I don't have a position in many specific areas. Because this is not about policymaking specifically in this forum. I am here to listen to your views, and if that is something that Singaporeans want to take up, maybe we have a conversation on that.

Chairperson: I am going to put that same question to the panel.

DC: Gender is a bit different from the other minority groupings, because half the world is male, the other half is female. Same for Singapore, whatever we say about dragon year babies, it is still about half. It is quite important to separate the two. In the United States, I happened to do research on these about the equal employment opportunities. Because of historical reasons they tend to put females and minorities together; because traditionally, [there are the] glass ceiling and biases. And the spirit of it is meritocracy and lack of biases. But psychologically and sociologically, females as a group is quite different from other minority groups. Earlier I gave the example of the Women's Charter. It is to highlight the fact that when you don't look at the group membership and group differences, certain policies will simply not occur. If I stopped seeing you as male or female there will never be a Women's Charter. My point was if I stopped seeing people as CMIO, or using the classification, I will not have the HDB quota system. We need to re-examine and say what policies do we really want to do away with, are you sure? That was where I was coming from.

A very quick point about group difference, because it keeps coming up. Whether it is LGBT, single mothers, abortions or other groupings, we want to recognise general group differences disagreement versus value differences that are fundamental. The government is in a tough position because we have LGBT groups on one side and religious groups on the other side. But we should not classify [it as] "Are you LGBT or not" because there are many people who are not LGBT who might support either group. Don't confuse your position with your group membership. But when there are value differences, what is important is, can you activate my different social identity? If you and I disagree on LGBT, surely you and I are more than our sexual orientations, are we not also Singaporeans? Do we not also believe in social harmony and respect for human dignity and if we do, instead of not talking about it, can we talk about it with these perimeters in mind? Can we talk about it that the moment it becomes exclusive. Why are we stopping the conversation? Because it is threatening social harmony. Why are we continuing the conversation? Because we respect human dignity. The decision to talk or not should be secondary, the core values and fundamentals should drive these value differences.

EH: I feel a little underrepresented here [as the only female on stage]. I am pretty sure I can hold my own. Perhaps rather than talk about specific identity categories, to follow up on what David was mentioning about talking about it and our core values. I am not sure I have caught fully what you said because the acoustics here are not great, but my key point here is that the very process of talking, that dialogue, shapes our core values. When it comes to diversity and hearing a diverse range of voices, the dialogue is essential. Where I am concerned is that, increasingly, we either see dialogues becoming very hotly contested and these cases, space for public debate has to be created. Where I am concerned is where these dialogues are taking place on cyberspace, because when they take place on cyberspace it is anonymous, and sometimes the views that are expressed tend to be of the vocal minority and the views expressed are quite extreme. I feel that going back to education, we need to educate our young people to be more competent in airing different voices, different points of views and engaging in balanced and reasoned debate, while remaining open to other people's points of views. Moving ahead, in terms of thinking how we cope with the growing diversity, that dialogue is important but the training that goes behind that dialogue is essential as well. If we talk about the education portfolio, I would like to see our teachers be better equipped to do this kind of diversity training. We see organisations hiring consultants to do diversity training and I think that our educators can be better equipped in this respect too — both pedagogically as well as in delivery.

NCM: Very good points made, and if you come back to the CMIO concept, Mr Ho Kwon Ping is quite exemplary in the discussion over time. I recall him saying about whether we need to nuance away or move away from CMIO conceptualisation, but when he had conversations with his minority friends, he heard the views of his friends that they still desire a structured representation in the politics of the day. He came up publicly and said that his viewpoint was perhaps not the most circumspect. That is conversation in forging cohesive diversity. I don't have a position that is consolidated and unchangeable. If there are better ways to view things, how can we accommodate and find the best way forward for our society? I fully agree with what David said. At a different level, I was having a conversation with Ms Teng [Siao See of IPS] just now because she is the expert in identity, how do we see ourselves as an individual, as a father, as a husband and so on and so forth, and actually in different conversations we assume different identities subconsciously? But if we are aware of bigger imperatives of ensuring that the society hold together in some of these thorny issues, then which identity can come forth to galvanise us and not let the disagreements pull us apart? I think that is the essence of how we see ourselves and the values that we uphold.

Q7: I want to point out that I don't think SAP schools begin at 14 years old and I am speaking as someone who went to an all-Chinese primary school — the school song was in Chinese, most of my teachers speak Chinese, so if you don't speak Chinese you cannot survive in the school. The only non-Chinese people were one Chindian boy and one *angmoh* girl, both of whom had Chinese as their mother tongue. I was in an all SAP school kid and this is an all SAP school kid from primary school to secondary school to JC. I would like to say, please do away with SAP schools because I wished that I had grown up, learnt with, played with and fought with people of different races and still had the same education, the same access to resources as I did in my SAP school education. That's my first point.

My second point is that I don't understand why we are constantly congratulating ourselves for the success of the CMIO model and wondering whether we should walk away from it in face of diversity when very obviously the CMIO model was actually a reductive model to begin with. Singapore has always been diverse, before 1965, after 1965. We are not getting more diverse, it is just that the old models are no longer working. Isn't it easier, instead of just constantly saying "CMIO", "not CMIO", why don't we just look at or learn from the problems of CMIO model and see how we can take this going forward? Perhaps the reason why a lot of Singaporeans have problems dealing with new alternatives or communities coming into Singapore is simply because we have been programmed, educated to think and reproduce these reductive categories of identity when relating to one another, instead of being taught or trained or educated or simply socialised to think in terms of individuals relating with one another and having the individual responsibility to relate with each other and constantly think.

It is not just about me being representative but who is being left out of any conversation that I happen to be in. Honestly if the Singapore education system, for all its efficacies, if it can be so good at producing a rational pragmatic Singaporean citizen like myself, who can still remember every single aspect of the National Education syllabus including things like we ourselves must rely on ourselves to succeed, no one else owes us a living — I can memorise everything about the reflection about all the wars, etc. — I think it can also be put in the education system to make us think about all these complexities in identities as well. It does no good to absolve government education system of the responsibility and just think that it is on the community, "it is for you guys to do". It is problematic to just reduce it between a false dilemma between CMIO or not.

NCM: Thank you very much for the passionate beliefs. Let me ask you a fundamental question: Is the issue borne out of a CMIO problem or borne out because humans organise ourselves with identities as the root problem? Which one came first? When we look at this issue, when we assume that the CMIO model is the root of the problem, then maybe we should do away with it, but when we came together in 1965 or maybe earlier, looked at the enclaves we had in Singapore. Even the Chinese were divided: Hokkien, Teochews, Cantonese, different enclaves. While, with the luxury of 50 years now, we say that you may need to rethink about the CMIO model, well without it, what would have happened? Would we have been able to pull ourselves together? Look at the rest of the world. Look at what's happening around us. I say this with humility that of course there are always better ways to do things, but have we done well in the last 50 years to forge such a disparate collection of people in this small little island Singapore without resources? Don't forget, in the 1960s, we were having difficulties making a living. In your generation, we are in a position of strength for us to have the luxury to have such a talk to forge our way forward. We also have the luxury of talented individuals like you that can think that can come together to find a way forward amidst the different challenges.

I am quite happy with your viewpoints that may not be in agreement with some of us, that's okay, let's find our way forward and this is really the spirit of cohesive diversity. I do not know whether you will be right in 10 years, 20 years' time, maybe the CMIO model with be obsolete. I look around in this room at us who are older, who also embrace the youthful idealism that you have, so that we ourselves don't get too cemented in our viewpoints. As I hear you, I will have to evaluate, with the passing of time, whether this would become the better way to think about things. Or should we still continue to lend tactical wisdom because we are somewhat older, lived through different things and seen different things. In that blending, how do we find the cohesive diversity as Singaporeans to chart the route forward? I am very willing to engage the younger groups I have always done that whether in the SAF or today, because you are the engine that will bring Singapore ahead with the idealism with the dare. My generation, at 47, we are sitting right about the inflection point, I will get more set in my ways as I get older, but I will fight that each and every day so that I can always listen to such articulate ideals of where we want to go as Singaporeans. Thank you very much for your comments.

HA: I think for cohesive diversity, with regard to inter-religious… back to the schools again, I think if we do not give the platform to be acquainted to one another's beliefs, then we will not understand each other and then we will not be able to appreciate. We should try to refrain from using the term tolerant, because it connotes some negativity in relationships. Moving forward when we talk about religious harmony, we should use what Janadas used about accepting our differences.

EH: We have covered quite a wide range of topics. Apart from talking about diversity, I want to reflect on what brings us together what enables us to communicate with one another as a nation, as people who live in Singapore. Part of it is having a common language like English, so that across different ethnic groups or languages we speak we are able to communicate. I also want to highlight that what makes Singapore quite unique is that we come from position of strength now, we have done well in many respects, other things we can do better, where we are now is that we can share this common vision of being future-oriented. In talking about the CMIO model, it has served us well, but moving forward how can we do better, reflecting on the different perspectives that have been brought in.

DC: Diversity is neutral, so is national identity — you can have bad national identity where we are in-group because we share a common enemy out-group such as the local-foreigner divide. If the only reason you like me as a Singaporean is because we have a common enemy, that is not going to work. The important part about identity is dealing with the differences to emerge and based on a common set of values. What we are relatively lacking in — we are okay with meritocracy and social harmony and other things — is social resilience, because we haven't had many setbacks, and the idea here is that when we quarrel, when we fail, when we have unmet expectations, can we still adhere to some of our common values and say it is okay let's bounce back? That part of the social resilience, we have not really quite been tested enough and so some of these little arguments and messiness maybe needs to occur under some controlled conditions, so that you can have some kind of resilience, I am not saying that please create a riot, don't misquote me, what I am saying is that when there is messiness actually there can be goodies out of messiness, if you know how to manage it. And for that to happen, understand that sometimes we need to annoy each other, government may annoy you but government needs to know that we might annoy the government as well.

NCM: Well the government won't ignore you. We listen. It is a very good discussion in my view. At the end of it, cohesive diversity, again, it is not just about the ideation in our conversations but subsequently after we leave this room, how would we behave as individuals, as leaders in society, as young people in society that will forge the way forward. When we talk about social diversity, our pledge can be copied around the world, any country can download our pledge, modify it and say that this is the vision. But why is it unique to Singapore that we have succeeded? It requires a clear vision to galvanise people together but it also requires unity of action amongst all of us, and agree that this is the broad vision we want to go forward under, whether it is a banyan tree or a tembusu tree that is flowered with orchids of different variations. How we chart a future to accommodate all the different viewpoints, that environment, the unity of action, is essential. And I put it as a concluding remark that the trust between the government and the people, the trust that my generation will have to earn in terms of integrity, competence and ability. And hopefully over time our track record will [let us] continue to enjoy this relationship, where inclusive politics will be a necessary environment where we have all these diverse viewpoints, agreements or disagreements — and in that conversation derive the energy, derive the strength to position Singapore forward for SG100.

3

Inclusive Growth?

Chairperson:
Vikram Khanna, Associate Editor, *The Business Times*

Speaker:
Ong Ye Kung (OYK), then Acting Minister for Education
(Higher Education and Skills)

Panel:
Yeoh Lam Keong (YLK), Adjunct Professor, Lee Kuan Yew School of
Public Policy

Chua Hak Bin (CHB), Head of ASEAN Economics, Bank of America
Merrill Lynch

Tan Kong Yam (TKY), Co-Director, Asia Competitiveness Institute,
Lee Kuan Yew School of Public Policy

OYK: I have always enjoyed attending Institute of Policy Studies (IPS)
Singapore Perspectives. When I was a civil servant, I got to attend and
would sit amongst you, listen and take notes. Thereafter, I could clock this
as training hours, which I have a target of 100 hours a year. Later on, I went
to the National Trades Union Congress (NTUC), and I still got to attend
and I never needed to take notes in NTUC. Then I joined a private
company — some of you would know, which is always the platinum
sponsor and we are treated so well at Perspectives. But I must say, these days
it is not as enjoyable coming to IPS Singapore Perspectives. I am always
somehow in the firing line.

And if my colleague Minister Heng Swee Keat is right, at some point in the next one-and-a-half hours, someone will say it all boils down to education. So we wait.

I would like to focus my speech squarely on the title, which is "Inclusive Growth" with a question mark. I think we all have an idea what inclusive growth is. So I'll talk about the question mark.

There are three possible questions. First, a question of definition. What does inclusive growth really mean? The second is a question of paradox. Can you have inclusivity and growth at the same time? Isn't it a tradeoff? Isn't it contradictory? And third is a more optimistic one. That if it is possible to have both, how do we achieve it?

First, on the definition of inclusive growth. We know what it is not. Growth without jobs cannot be inclusive growth because workers do not benefit from such growth. It also cannot be growth that is concentrated entirely at the top.

Today the overall theme is the concept of "we". Some of the speakers had used the pledge, which I will also use. The Singapore pledge has two important words — "justice and equality". I think our concept of inclusive growth revolves around these two powerful words. And our pledge went further to explain why justice and equality. It is "so as to achieve happiness, prosperity and progress for our nation." I think this is our collective aspiration for Singaporeans, and our definition of inclusive growth.

Second is the question of the paradox. It is very relevant because there is indeed a tension between inclusivity and growth. This is why the way we measure growth and inclusivity is problematic. Let's start with growth. We measure growth by GDP per capita, which is a very flawed concept.

The numerator GDP itself does not measure welfare. Many things that make us happy and give us welfare cannot be measured or bought by money. Let me give an example. If you and I eat the dinner we cook for ourselves, there is no GDP. If you exchange our dinners, suddenly there is GDP because it becomes tradable. And chances are welfare may actually drop because I may not like your cooking and you may not like mine. GDP has its limits. It was essentially created in the 1930s by John Maynard Keynes who used it as a way to measure the aggregate demand for tradable, monetisable goods and services.

And if you look at the denominator — per capita, we all know the problem of averages. It doesn't measure the variance and disparity of income, which is a concern many of us will have.

The other alternate measurement of inclusivity is the Gini coefficient, which is also flawed. Many of us would know if the Gini coefficient is zero, it means everybody earns the same income. When it is one, it means one person earns everything. China has lifted hundreds of millions of Chinese out of poverty over the last 30 years, but at a cost of rising Gini coefficient. So is it good or is it bad? But to be fair, China's efforts have allowed the world's Gini coefficient to come down.

Take another simple example. A family with members that are all unemployed has a Gini coefficient of zero. But If one person finds a job, it shoots to one. So which is better?

In addition, inequality today is not just between the middle income and lower income. In fact, the issue is now between the top 1% and the rest of the masses. It goes beyond just income disparity, but is also about the power that comes with the money at the top. When we see the kind of money and campaign funding that goes into lobbying in some political systems, it calls into question the whole legitimacy and credibility of the government.

Having said all that, numbers are up to us to use. We can still use the numbers that are relevant, but must bear in mind their limitations.

The last question is about getting there. Here I will use the pledge again. There are many things we can do and I'll categorise them into three groups of measures: Happiness, prosperity and progress. I will describe them in reverse order, starting with progress.

PROGRESS

I think a big part of progress is social progress, and the starting point is to keep our tax system light for the average worker, and at the same time, progressive. Singapore has done fairly well on this: 55% of Singaporeans do not pay taxes; and the top 20% of Singaporeans pay 55% of all the taxes. The average tax burden on the average Singapore worker is only 2%, compared with 36% in Denmark and 23% in Finland.

Second are the social programmes. I do not want to give a laundry list of social programmes we have, but over the last 10 years a lot has been done. The GST Voucher has cushioned the impact of GST on the lower-income.

There are also many other social programmes that help out with housing, transport and medical care, such as the Pioneer Generation Package, or PGP, and MediShield Life. And when workers have problems, they can undergo training and re-training, and receive ComCare assistance. Because of all these efforts in social redistribution, today for every dollar a middle-income worker pays, he gets back S$2 of benefits. For a lower-income worker, for every dollar of tax he pays, he gets back S$6.

Education and training is also an important part of progress. Education is such a critical social leveller, and we must make sure that we get our education system right and world-class. Today, Institute of Technical Education (ITE), polytechnics and autonomous universities take in about 90% of each cohort. Over the years, the Ministry of Education has monitored and measured starting salaries to make sure that our higher education system continues to produce students that are relevant to the economy and valued by industry. If you look at average starting salaries for ITE in the last five years, it has increased from S$1,500 to S$1,800. Polytechnic students, post-NS (National Service), earn from S$2,000 to S$2,400. For university graduates, it is S$2,700 to S$3,200. They have all increased; even if you take into account inflation, there are still some real increases. This is possible only if the economy continues to grow, which leads me to prosperity.

PROSPERITY

Economic growth is critical. We no longer have the high single-digit growth that we used to enjoy, but we can continue to have steady and modest single digit growth. Growth has delivered higher real incomes for Singaporeans. From 2004 to 2014, real individual income after taxes and transfers at the 20th percentile has increased 14.8%; at the median it is a bit more at 21.4%. If you take real household increase in income over the last 10 years after taxes and transfers, the number is 45% for the bottom 20%, and at the median, 38%. Compare these numbers with other economies — the US, the UK, Hong Kong, Taiwan, and you will find that they are in negative territory or only slightly positive.

The combination of progress and prosperity allows social mobility. For students that used to be in the bottom 20th percentile households and in their late 20s and 30s, a good proportion of them moved up to the top 20% of households. The number is in fact 14.3% — not bad at all.

But of course, our economy is at the verge of needing further transformation. It is a bit like Walt Disney. It used to market Mickey Mouse and Donald Duck; today it is in Marvel superheroes and Star Wars. The Singapore economy likewise has to go through such a transformation to be more attractive and competitive. This is a big topic that the Committee of Future Economy (CFE) will have to discuss over the next one year. But we see some of the vision in the initiatives already coming out. SkillsFuture is one, the Research, Innovation and Enterprise 2020, or RIE2020, that has committed S$19 billion for the next five years, is another. These are all significant strategies to transform our economy and we will discuss this at the CFE.

Whatever it is, we need to bear in mind that many of us in this room, barring the students, have established careers and sometimes can afford to talk about inclusivity and redistribution. But amongst the young, the undergrads, polytechnic graduates, their biggest concern is their jobs and careers, and if there are sufficient opportunities for them. We cannot fail the young.

HAPPINESS

The last category of measures is happiness. I use this to broadly describe everything that is less tangible and has to do with the heart. One important part is philanthropy and volunteerism. We can have income disparity, but if people at the top volunteer to help, and people with wealth participate in philanthropy, we can narrow the psychological disparity.

The second part is social behaviour. All our measures to help uplift the lower income and vulnerable require the collaboration and cooperation of the whole society. I just read *The Straits Times* this morning — we are going to raise the fines for people who park in disabled lots. This is really sad. Why should someone even think of parking in a disabled lot? We can set aside resources and space to help the vulnerable, but if other people misuse it, our effort comes to naught. Social cohesiveness is hence important.

As another example, as Members of Parliament, we look at various improvements in our community. Sometimes I would suggest building a ramp or a path outside a HDB block so that it would be easier for the elderly to walk to the bus stop or the coffeeshop. Often HDB would advise me against it, because the ramp or path is directly under the windows, and they did not want the elderly to be harmed by killer litter. There should be more social pressures against such acts. The same goes for funding schemes. The more abuse there is, the less goes towards the lower income.

Lastly, happiness is also about choice. Over the past 10 years, the government has done a lot and many people have described that as a move to the left. But if you look further left, there are still many policies on the table. For example, a national minimum wage as opposed to a sectoral minimum wage, unemployment insurance, or the definition of absolute poverty and helping Singaporeans below that definition to reach a certain subsistence of living and income. On the extreme right, there are also policies such as further restricting foreign immigrants, or nationalising some of our companies and making them contribute to national coffers.

While these policies are still on the table, we do not move left for the sake of moving left, and move right for the sake of moving right. We decide on what policies will best serve the welfare of our people, and help us achieve that elusive inclusive growth. Ultimately such choices are moral and political ones, and require collective decisions; which is why they are often contested.

Whatever the outcome of a contest, the people of Singapore will decide what package of measures is best for us, and where we stand in the whole spectrum. And whatever our choices, we must live with it, be satisfied with it, and be contented with it. With contentment, we get happiness; with happiness, we can then have progress and prosperity for our nation.

Thank you very much.

Chairperson: Thank you, Minister Ong, for flagging and raising a rich array of issues. You asked whether there is a tension between inclusivity and growth and mentioned the top 1% issue. But generally I get the feeling that Singapore is doing alright in terms of inclusiveness. You talked about the effectiveness of the redistributive programme that Singapore has put in place. You also talked about decent increase in incomes for the bottom and the middle level income of the population, and social mobility being quite good in Singapore. What does the panel think about Minister Ong's comments?

YLK: Thank you, Minister Ong. Always a pleasure to listen to your views. I agree with a lot of them, in particular your broad approach of focusing on the three the words in the pledge that have eluded economics and economic policies for a long time — happiness, progress and prosperity, and in the particular, the combination of all three. I would add a fourth word reflected in today's theme, "we", which refers to us Singaporeans. If we combine these four words, "we", "happiness", "prosperity" and "progress", we begin to get to what good economic and inclusive policies should be about.

Inequality has become a huge issue. The experience of most people in developed countries, including Singapore, has led to the rising importance of inequality. We are not just talking about the widening disparity between income groups. We are talking about that plus the fact that for the average person in the economy, they have been experiencing slow to stagnating wages for a decade. I know we've got 1–2% real wage growth in the last 10 years, but this is insufficient when you are bringing up your family and when you have aspirations of a middle class. Wages are now positive but for decades there was depression of wages at the bottom 20%. This is happening not just in Singapore but worldwide. It has to do with global factors, such as technology, the displacement of labour and policies.

In Singapore, we have to admit that one of the main economic models that have gone wrong for 20 years has been our goal for cheap, labour-intensive growth policy, which encouraged periods of low wage erosion and wage stagnation. This policy based on 3–4% labour force growth, largely fuelled by immigration, brought our population from 3 million in 1995 to 5.5 million today. The result is depressed wages and productivity. It is probably one of the bigger policy errors we have. Luckily, we recognise this. Although the Economic Strategies Committee has been moving towards productivity-driven growth since 2010, but its after-effects remain: We have created a starting level where our wages at the bottom 20% are far below than those in comparative GDP per capita countries like Hong Kong. We have also created a social-economic time bomb because if we cannot slow our labour force growth to genuine productivity growth that is below 1%, then by 2050, we are going to end up with a population far above seven million and that will lead to an economy that will looks more Dubai's than Switzerland. It will have profound impact not just on overall welfare and well-being but also on social cohesiveness — the sense of "we" that should be the raison d'être of public policy. This was not addressed at all in the Population White Paper.

Inclusive growth includes social policies and I would like to name six key policies for the Minister's consideration and ask particular questions about them: First, social security including poverty and retirement adequacy; second, affordable public housing; third, proper universal long-term care and chronic primary care system vital for our rapidly ageing population; fourth, egalitarian education; fifth, improving infrastructure and public transport; sixth, population and immigration policies. These are key areas that if provided properly do a great deal for the sense happiness, prosperity and progress that we all desire. The government needs to do some heavy lifting in these areas.

In the first 30 years of our independence we did this very well. We had universal healthcare and egalitarian education that brought us to mobility levels close to Germany. We had affordable housing and were able to pay them off in 10 years. We had strong rising family incomes relative to desired goods and we were very careful about excess immigration. Dr Goh Keng Swee scolded us harshly if we dared to suggest that Singapore should have anything like the immigration levels we have today. Lee Kuan Yew himself had said that 4–5 million people is his preferred level of final population in Singapore. However, things have changed and there were big shifts in policies in which we became much more market-oriented in the way we provided these goods.

Housing became more unaffordable and healthcare became more un-affordable for the poor, but now we are reversing policies with MediShield Life. Education became effectively privatised with less mobility. Cars are unaffordable, but public transport is nowhere as good as Hong Kong's. The depression of wages has become a problem again by most measurements — 10–12% of resident households are in that category. And the population problem. All these things collectively threaten well-being, cohesion, national identity, prosperity, progress, happiness and our sense of "we". This is our nation — neither a hotel nor a long-term home, but is this where we would be happy to see our kids and grand kids settle?

I would to ask these six questions. Can the government as part of inclusive growth commit to achieving key long-term targets in these six areas: One, decisively abolish poverty and achieve decent retirement adequacy. Two, can we achieve affordable public housing payable to maximum 10–15 years, and supplement that by an adequate supply of decent affordable rental housing? Three, can we have affordable, universal and long-term chronic healthcare in addition to just hospitalisation? Four, can we have educational reforms to give more priority to social mobility, creativity and initiative-heavy and tuition-light system? Five, can we please have at least a Hong Kong standard level of public transport? Six, can we please commit to the Prime Minister's stated population target in Parliament of well below 6.9 million?

Thank you.

Chairperson: Thank you, Lam Keong. Well, since you have covered a lot of ground and ask some very pointed questions, I should give the Minister an opportunity respond.

OYK: Thank you, Lam Keong. If we ever have debates, I would think that Lam Keong and I would be mostly on the same side.

It is hard to argue against the aspirations of the six policies whether it is better public transport, universal healthcare that is affordable, and affordable housing. These are all original aspirations of the PAP government and we must continue to work on them. I just want to point out that the kind of measures, grants, help given to especially lower income households over the last few years have been able to achieve all aims.

We do a lot of block visits. One of the most satisfying experiences of any block visit is when you ask a family, "Where do you used to live?", and they say "I lived in a rental flat", but are able to slowly paying off and starting to own their two or three-room flats even though they do not earn a lot now (about S$1,200–S$1,500). That is the most satisfying. This shows that policies are filtering down to the ground and helping families and children own a home. I believe policies are working on the ground.

But I also want to point out that as we do this, there must also be growth. For many of the lower-income, the best way to help them is actually by ensuring that they have a better job and are equipped with skills. I was in the union in four years, and I always remember one incident. When I visited various bus interchanges, one bus driver told me, "I earn S$1,250 and long hours" — that was probably in 2008. He added, "I don't want handouts. I want better recognition for the work and the job scope that I am doing. I am responsible for lives. Give me a better pay so I can stand on my own." His words guided my four years of working at NTUC. Those in the bus unions know what we have done — we spent three years negotiating with two bus operators and today we have much better starting pay. I believe now it is at S$1,650 or even higher. I think these are the important things.

I want to make one more important point. Lam Keong mentioned abolishing absolute poverty. I agree with that as a concept. We want to do that. But from a practical point of view, poverty is also relative. Residents have different difficulties, so sometimes it is difficult to judge and judgement is indeed needed. I met one Uber driver who is earning S$2,000–S$3,000 a month, but he has six schooling children to support and it is very tough. Someone else would have a different story. A single who lives on his or her own and earns S$1,500. To decide who is the poorer of the two, you need to take into account the burden that is on them. There are even PMETs that are earning S$5,000–S$6,000 with two cancer-stricken parents. How do you judge who needs more? It is not easy to define absolute poverty and say that we are going to eradicate it.

We also need to take into consideration people's desire to stand on their own two feet. I have an experience with a mother and son that come to my Meet-the-People session every week without fail. The mother is a very hardworking old lady who works odd jobs to support the son. The son is healthy (around 40 years old), but simply refuses to work and is often drinking. How do we help? Both are jobless and have no income. As an exercise of judgement, we do whatever we can to help the mother. We tell the son to keep looking for a job and offer to train him. There are such practical implementation issues on the ground. Poverty and low-income are real, but to abolish absolute poverty through a formula is not easy to implement. A lot of things need to be done on the ground.

Chairperson: Thank you, Mr Minister. If we may now move on to Hak Bin for his comments?

CHB: Thank you, Vikram. I have two points. Lam Keong has mentioned all the key concerns and I cannot dispute about wanting more affordable housing, better public transport and healthcare, and higher wages. But today we are coming at a time when growth is struggling in Singapore so I am going to talk a bit about the tradeoffs.

The job growth last year is 30,000 — down from 130,000 the previous year, which is 80%, so I'm not sure if the graduates this year will have an easy time. It's not just Singapore that is going through this bad patch. Then there is some impact from restructuring, so we have to ask whether the policies have in some way contributed to worsening the slowdown.

The markets are now pricing in a recession and we seemed to have just narrowly slipped one. Standard economics textbooks will tell you growth and inequality are separate objectives, and if you maximise efficiency growth that would be the best outcome. If the outcome is unequal, you can effect lump-sum transfers of income to help the lower-income that has been left out, so I would use polices like Central Provident Fund (CPF) top-up, the wage credit schemes, the housing grants and the Pioneer Generation Package to achieve a more equal outcome. The second category of policies that try to achieve better efficient growth outcome would include the SkillsFuture, the Productivity and Innovation Credit scheme, and perhaps the S$19-billion R&D scheme that just has been proposed. These schemes try to push the growth boundary.

But in reality, it is probably difficult to achieve a cost-less redistribution. Taxes or interventionist policies that have been introduced to influence prices, wages and assets. The question is whether some of these more intrusive or "protectionist" policies that have come at the expense of growth. In this group, I would also include the following policies: Foreign manpower policies and their quotas and higher taxes. And even property measures, which has a social objective and is no longer just a financial stability objective.

The economy is slowing down. The potential growth four years ago was 5%, but it has since decreased. We hope we can achieve 2% this year. The first question is: Have these interventionist policies shifted so much left at the expense of growth that it will hurt the ability to effect redistributional policies?

As a market economist, I would like to get a sense of what policies have an impact on growth, if any. With the SkillsFuture scheme and the likes of it, it is very hard to get excited on the ultimate impact on growth. This is an expanded version of the post-secondary scheme and it is very hard to quantify its results. A case in point is the Productivity and Innovation Credit (PIC) scheme. We spent S$3–S$4 billion on the scheme, but when you look at the numbers, private investment has been contracting for over two years. Why has it failed to support or revive private investments when the government is willing to fund so much and co-share some of the risks? Why has labour productivity growth continue to be in the negative for the fourth year running despite some of the policies that have tried to encourage productivity? This is a bit of a worry. We have also pumped in S$19 billion into an R&D scheme, which is a lot of money and twice as much money spent on the Pioneer Generation scheme. How do we measure the outcome and make sure that the money is well spent in that category? It is hard to capture the improvements in the R&D sector.

Chairperson: Thank you, Hak Bin. Minister, would you like to comment on those points, particularly the point that you have so many schemes some of which are not working as intended?

OYK: In the interest of time, why don't we let Kong Yam say his piece and…

Chairperson: Sure, Kong Yam, please.

TKY: I agree with Lam Keong in some of the points and even though I am sitting to his left, my assessment is not farther left because if I were to go further left I might fall off the stage. I like to look at income inequality and inclusive growth from a slightly different perspective. In the last decade, wage stagnation and the inequality of the young people in Korea, Taiwan and Hong Kong are becoming a very serious socio-political problem; as you are aware, Korea has riots, Taiwan has the sunflower movement even though it is partly China linked — but a lot of it is actually the inequality and frustration with young people. Hong Kong had the famous umbrella movement. In Singapore, we have not yet had an orchid flower movement. This is partly because the government is quite effective, but I would venture to argue that it is also due to certain structures in our system. We should make sure that we sustain this system and do not tinker with it. With globalisation rapidly evolving and technological changes becoming more rapid, a city-state like Singapore, with our bell-shape distribution of income, the lower end [of income] is pulled down by regional countries' lower wages because some of the factories can relocate to regional countries where cost is lower even if we don't bring in cheaper foreign workers. At the upper end of the bell shape curve we've got people like Chua Hak Bin who works for Bank of America, whose salary is pulled up by New York. We cannot resist these forces because we are too small. So what is the solution? I do not think it is [having] a lot of welfare... for a sustainable way to reduce our social tension and inequality, and ensure inclusive growth for all Singaporeans, we should manage it from the consumption side. What do I mean by that? If I am a household that earns S$70,000 a year and Chu Hak Bin earns S$280,000, which is four times above mine — the inequality is very wide. We have a city-state structure and we can ensure that even though the gross income inequality is high, our effective income inequality is low. Not just through the transfer or welfare that Lam Keong mentioned, but more in terms of three critical policies.

First, housing. I may be earning S$70,000 per household a year, but If I stay in a four-room flat in Jurong West, which costs S$490,000, I use seven years of my income to get decent housing. Chua Hak Bin goes for a S$2 million condo, which is equivalent to his seven years' income. So our effective Gini coefficient is not that high. If you include that into public transport and private transport — he drives a BMW, I take the Mass Rapid Transit (MRT) and occasionally taxis, the disparity is also high. If he goes for private hospital and if I go for public hospital, our effective income inequality in terms of consumption bundle and purchasing power is not that significantly different. This means that at the fundamental level, our system should use land as an indirect transfer. All of us work hard, we generate GDP growth, we generate wealth and everything. The biggest beneficiary of this wealth is the big boss, which is the government. They own a lot of land. The land price appreciates by using public housing subsidised land on public housing. Public transport is also land-related, because Certificate of Entitlement (COE) is a congestion cost on land scarcity. So if we use land to subsidise these key items — transport and housing, we are able to ensure low income inequality without giving everybody a lot of *ang pow* every day. Now this is not a trivial matter.

As some of you remember, from 2008 to 2011 our Housing & Development Board (HDB) resale price went up enormously, and I estimated that, for the general election vote that declined from 2006 (66%) to 2011 (60%), half of the 6 percentage-point decrease was due to escalating housing cost. With the eventual reversal of housing price, from 60% in General Elections (GE) 2011 to almost 70% in GE 2011, out of the 10 percentage-point improvement the performance, four percentage points are due to housing. This is a significant impact. One of the reasons why we do not have an orchid flower movement is actually due to this. When you talk to young people in Korea, Hong Kong and Taiwan, you can see this effect clearly. I have a question after the comment. We realise that as we move ahead, innovation is an important driving force for productivity — and that is the key part. And our recently National Research Foundation (NRF) plan of S$19 billion is pushing on that. One of the Economic Intelligence Unit (EIU) studies measures 24 countries on their innovation input and innovation output. Innovation input means how much R&D per GDP, how many engineers you train, how much IP protection, etc. On the output side, it measures how many patents per capita you generate, the level of technological sophistication of your exports, the firm's technological level and how far it is from the world technology frontier. And then they divide innovation output by the innovation input to get an efficiency ratio. That means like if you put meat, *sambal,* curry powder into a grinder and grind, how much sausage comes out? In Singapore's case, our input ranks at number one, we put in a lot of curry powder and meat, but our output does not rank so high. So our efficiency ratio is number 10 out of 24. Not only is our efficiency ratio ranked below Finland, Japan and the US, it is actually ranked below Korea, Taiwan and Hong Kong. I would like to get the Minister's view, as he is also a member of the NRF, on how Singapore can improve its efficiency ratio over the next five to 10 years, because this is very critical for our future productivity improvement.

OYK: First, thanks for the panellists' views. Kong Yam seems to have a model of election outcomes. Can I please borrow that? I appreciate that all three panellists have acknowledged how much the government has done in terms of social transfers. Kong Yam gave a refreshing view on our Gini coefficient and how to interpret it. I think for Kong Yam and Hak Bin, the fundamental point they are making is that they are worried about our economic future. I do remember that last week when I was reading *The Business Times*, Hak Bin was on the front page as usual — he was mentioning that he was worried about the Committee of Future Economy, whether we will just end up tinkering and not doing something bold that can transfer us, just like Walt Disney transformed from Mickey Mouse to Star Wars. That is also my key worry.

I want to explain it like that. If you look at Hong Kong and Taiwan today, both are having deep problems, they are opposite from one another, but equally deep. Hong Kong has lost its industrial base and is relying completely on services. And when it is facing more competition from Shanghai and the like, it finds itself too single-dimensional as an economy. Two days ago, CY Leung made a policy speech on that saying that Hong Kong must regain its industrial base, because without it, it loses a scientific base. Without a scientific base, you can't have innovation. That's the problem for Hong Kong that has led to its stagnation. Taiwan has the opposite problem. It held on to its industrial base, so it is still manufacturing. But it is also facing tremendous competition from China and all these industrial bases. Unlike Hong Kong, Taiwan did not develop a vibrant services sector. And today, it is also finding itself single-dimensional, and so it is also facing a problem. So opposite positions, but similar problems.

In our case, it is not too bad. Singapore has 19% of our GDP from manufacturing and we have a growing services sector. In fact I would argue that many of our services sector leverage on our manufacturing expertise and scientific base in order for them to grow — IT and power for examples. We are in a fairly not-too-bad position to work from. How do we go from here? Recently a professor from the US told me that Detroit went down and in fact the city has gone bankrupt because it focused on the manufacturing of cars, but really there was no innovation. The nearest research university is Michigan, which is too far away. On the other hand, Pittsburgh, which was a steel town is booming because of Carnegie Mellon, and many tech giants such as Google are hiring graduates from there. And today I was told that Google's second biggest campus in the world is in Pittsburgh. So the city has a revival — from a steel maker into an IT base city. So we must make sure that RIE 2020 ensures that we hold on to that scientific industrial base, and continue to drive innovation. On that point, I absolutely agree with Kong

Yam that we must find a way to translate research into innovation and innovation into enterprise. Research converts money into discovery; innovation converts discovery into business ideas; enterprise converts business idea back to money — hopefully more than when you first started. So we have to push forward. If there are any papers — Kong Yam, you've analysed input and output ratios — how we can do these better? NRF is more than happy to rope you in to continue this work.

QUESTION AND ANSWER SESSION

Q1: I am Phua Kai Hong from the Lee Kuan Yew School of Public Policy. I teach social policy and health policy. Not very much has been covered on the ground of health so I assume everything is okay here. We did talk about the dirty word "welfare", but I suppose this topic, when you put a question mark to the title "inclusive growth", concerns the big tradeoff between efficiency and equity, and you can't have distribution unless you can grow, which you all agree. But the kind of distribution that we hear about tonight — and like Kong Yam's proposal, it is not all about income distribution — it is about the distribution of the benefits basically on the consumption side. And this is where we have to be mindful about what type of equity we are talking about. Perhaps we might even have to change the word or definition of equality; that it is not equality for its own sake but it is basically a concept of Rawlsian equity. It is about equal access and equal chances and opportunities. You can't be equal; we are born unequal. We can't hope to have the same equal outcomes of everything, but yet we should give everybody a level playing field. We should strive to it but we cannot have perfect equality. It can be based on your means and your needs. We need to have a big debate about "Is it equality of allocation, is it equality of access or utilisation or outputs or outcomes?" When we talk about different sectors, again the needs are very different. So we look at health for example, we seem to have solved the problem by having MediShield Life and the Pioneer Generation Package, but we have really looked at the supply side, looked at where the benefits are going to accrue, looked at private vs. public? And here is where the whole issue of allocative efficiency comes in. That would define then your equity. If you are not doing too much in terms of the efficiency....

Chairperson: Sorry, sorry, could you come to your question?

Q1 (cont'd): So the question I have is: We don't seem to be clear about what our transaction cost, dimension cost is in the process of converting from an allocation efficiency to an equity, so we are straddled in this input-output thing to say that, well Singapore is not that efficient, we seem to be putting a lot of inputs but not getting outputs. Because of our allocation, there may be some inefficiency, there are some welfare losses. I don't know if the thing we are tinkering around with, is it translating to the kind of outcomes — better health, better happiness, better welfare. That is my question.

Chairperson: Thank you. Would Kong Yam like to deal with that since he mentioned your input-output allocation?

TKY: He has a lot of points. What I am mentioning is that actually our public housing and public transport and public health system are a very, very important policy for social stability. And it doesn't have as much distortion on incentive as very big welfare structures. In terms of health, actually the public health system is quite focused on the low-middle income group. You know I once had a gall bladder inflammation. So I went to National University Hospital (NUH). At first they thought it was some serious problem, so they examined and [found out that] it was not so serious. So they pushed me aside, then there were a lot of other people who came in later than me. And they all got attended earlier than me even though I was in the A class [ward] and they were the B2/C class [wards]. So I asked the staff, and the explanation was a very good one: Since my case is not as serious, and some of the other cases, even though they are B2 or C, are more serious than me in terms of urgency, so they pushed me aside. At first I didn't quite like it, but later I thought it through, and our public health system does have a certain levelling effect. And I think that public housing and transport have that similar situation. And it is important to actually maintain that especially for public housing because we have to make sure that public housing is actually a home [and] not an escalating asset. And I think that is what changed after GE 2011 — this is an important thing that should be maintained otherwise it could create serious problems. If you talk to young people in Hong Kong, Taiwan and Korea, without a big public housing system this is one of the serious sources of instability.

OYK: I will make a couple of comments. I think the key question is allocation inefficiency, which I think is something you always have to watch. I have come to the conclusion that to ensure that we are allocating resources and producing the right results, the biggest factor is people. You've got to hand it to the right person who can move the team and implement it effectively. And be very real about it, not just come up with indicators that say that these are all done because the indicators say so. You must reach out to the ground; you must make sure it works. As a young civil servant when I first joined, I heard so many stories of Mr Lee Kuan Yew who would just haul up a minister or a civil servant and say "I want to achieve this, you go and do it", and somehow the person would run around until they achieved it. I think that this is the kind of spirit we need to have within the system: Take the resources and believe passionately in it, and then achieve it.

On healthcare specifically, it can be a lot more efficient. The key issue is really having the right facilities. Today, we are still very much biased towards acute health hospitals. But really, many patients ought to be in community hospitals, and some maybe just [near facilities] where they are upstairs and they can come down where there are facilities for them to spend a few hours with nurses there who can attend to them. You look at the resources, in the acute care hospitals, it is six workers to one bed. In a community care hospital, it is two healthcare workers to one bed. And in the nursing home it is the other way round, one worker to six beds. So we need to move towards having more facilities that are in the community, so that there is proper stepdown care, and not have everyone deployed into the acute care hospitals take up resources. That would be an inefficient allocation of resources.

YLK: Quick comment here. Again we find ourselves on the same page, Minister Ong and Kong Yam. I agree that healthcare, housing and transport are actually three of the key six areas that I mentioned just now. And my comment here is in agreement. We have the resources to do it. Why? Government owns 80% of the land in Singapore, unlike many other countries where they don't even own 10% of the land. We already own it because of previous land reform policies already carried out by the government. This is our inalienable and tremendous asset of which we should use fully for social policy in a rational way. The question is: Are we fully utilising it as best we can? It is the sum and substance of housing policy — housing that was once possible to be paid off in 10–15 years even in the early years of independence. And then after the experimentation of linking BTO prices to resale prices, it went up to 20–30 years. Now we are back down to 15–20 years. Can we push it back to 10–15 years? Yes we can. We own the land. It doesn't cost us that much. So are we going to do it? Can we also provide the related rental housing, which is needed by people right at the bottom that cannot afford to buy? Yes we can. As Kong Yam says, it would be a transfer that does not disincentivise working effort. It gives everyone a stake. Why don't we do it? Same for public transport. Here I totally agree with the Minister. It is totally a question of the incentive and team. Why is SMRT a public-listed company? Public-listed companies incentivise short-term price-earnings ratios on the stock market. But you can keep it publicly listed; we can just make sure that you have dominant ownership, like they do it in Hong Kong. Is that a better alignment of corporate interest that will serve the commuter first rather than just the shareholders? That is a big question. Yes we can. We have the facilities, we have the ownership already; most of the profits already goes to Temasek. Yes we can.

Similarly for healthcare, I agree that community-based service is exactly the way to go. We have achieved wonderfully with MediShield Life, universal healthcare in acute health. Can we now go on to provide it in long-term care and chronic healthcare? As of now, Singapore has very little, virtually no long-term healthcare infrastructure compared to say even Hong Kong, where within 1 km of a residential area there is an eldercare centre that is affordable. Can we go on to do that? Yes we can.

Chairperson: Thank you, Lam Keong. If we can, I think we can also give the audience a chance to ask some more questions.

Q2: So far in the conference, I think we have paid very little attention to what I think are two major challenges in Singapore. First, I think there is a huge underbelly of local SMEs whose productivity is very low. And much has been done for them, or many policies have been developed for them. But I don't know whether up until now have they truly benefited or have been helped by the kind of growth that Singapore has. And I am not talking about the dynamic innovative companies that have sprung up in Singapore — all those are very good. I am not talking about the local big companies nor about the MNCs. This is really about those hundreds and thousands of small local SMEs. The second question pertains not only to inclusive growth, but also about the diversity we have — harmonious diversity, cohesive diversity — and that is to a segment of the population that is fast becoming the silver-hair generation. It is not just a question of providing for them in terms of CPF, savings and financially, etc., but it is also about how they are accepted in both the economy as well as the society. For example, an older person naturally speaks slower, thinks slower, talks slower, not to say that we don't have any ideas to give, but I think that there is a difference in the productivity of the older generation compared to that of the young. And it is not just an issue of raising the [retirement] age to 67, but it is a question that how as a society that is rapidly ageing, are we going to accommodate, first and foremost an economic dependency ratio that is going down to very low levels very quickly? And second, how are we, in terms of values, accommodating the ageing generation?

OYK: These are two of the toughest questions. Silver-hair generation. For many years I ran the outfit called the Employment and Employability Institute, where we try, through training and employment facilitation, to help the unemployed find jobs. And I must say that middle-aged PMEs as well as the silver-haired are the hardest to place. Sometimes, it is "tails I win, heads you lose". Because when they go for an interview, if they say "I used to be the manager or I used to head an office and this is my salary", the employer will say that you are asking for too much so I can't employ you. And if after much counselling they change and are prepared to take a pay cut, employers may ask, "What's wrong with you? Why are you taking a pay cut?" Both ways they lose, and I think a lot has to do with the entire business community, especially also the HR practice. We have to be very mindful of this issue. There are of course difficulties and conflict when the young and old work together. But we've just got to deal with it. We have to learn to deal with it. The young have to learn how to work with older people, and older people have to learn how to work with younger people. And I think some are trying. Young people are like cash, there is a lot of currency in what they just learnt. But older people are just like stored value cards, where the value is there but you must have the right interface to tap in, and that requires a new form of HR practice. As a start, never sort applications by age; no matter how thick the application stack is, don't sort by age. I will recommend that one don't even sort by class of honours or anything like that. You may need to have some form of sorting, and after that really interview the person to know what the person's strength is and then hire on that basis. And until we reach there, the government will not be able to solve the problem.

As for SMEs, they account for two-thirds of our employment so they are absolutely important. But SMEs are often lower in productivity, not across all sectors but in many sectors. And at the same time, increasingly, they may not be able to compete. But on the other hand — just now I was mentioning about Taiwan, Hong Kong and Singapore, we actually have quite a diversified economy. But it also means that it is quite hard for the Committee of Future Economy, compared to the past, to declare that "this is the growing sector, government is putting money into it, and let's all go into this sector, and if you are young, go and study in this sector." It is quite difficult to do that, because I think we have become quite diversified, and so somewhere, at some point of our economy, we must be able to allow bottom-up innovation and bottom-up discovery of our strengths rather than top-down from the government to declare that "this is the sector I am going to invest in and grow." And if we have a more bottom-up driven economic growth, I think that bodes well for the SMEs; not all, but I think innovation can be rewarded.

We are seeing a great change in the economic configuration of Asia. What is this change? In the past, if you are like Hong Kong and Taiwan, you look at China's value chain, and you plug into it and say that you play there, and you can earn a good living. And we did so, because it is a big production space, we can contract out manufacturing work into China. Today if you do that, you are quite dead, because the value chain now is dictated by China, and you cannot compete with Shanghai, even in the West, or the production centres. We now have to look at the entire value chain and say that this is a huge business space, a huge consumer market for us to tap into — and that opens up lots of opportunities for SMEs. And in the CFE these are some of the issues that we have to address.

Q3: All of the debate so far on inclusive growth has not really talked about education. So my question is related to education, specifically relating to the concept of degree inflation. I think I speak on the behalf of the people of my age and my juniors, who feel that without a degree in Singapore, it is basically impossible to experience growth in social mobility in the middle class in the future. So my question is, as we move forward and transform our economy, is there a future where my younger cousins won't feel the need to have a degree, and their parents won't say, "Regardless of what you do, please get a degree before you go out to work"?

OYK: I hope that whatever changes that come, it will not affect your cousins but will affect you too because you still have a long way ahead in your career. I think I wouldn't say that you do not need a degree. I think that many parents and many students aspire to have a degree, and I don't think we should kill those aspirations, and tell them you don't have to have a degree. But we must, before asking them to have a degree, ask them first what are their aspirations? What is the area of specialisation that you are interested in, or even better, passionate in? Or you know something about it, and you are prepared to cultivate passion as you go in. Because until we all find our specialty, invest and dedicate effort — sometimes throughout our whole life to develop that specialty, do we become excellent and gain mastery. And that is when we become competitive. That is when SMEs can be innovative and SMEs can be productive. There is no shortcut. You have to spend your whole life working in one area, to become good at it. And so the worry about degree is not so much about people wanting a degree, but the fact that there is no perseverance and no resilience. After picking an area, let's say in polytechnic I pick an area and I know something about it, and next thing I switch because I want a degree and I pick something else, usually a softer science subject. That is why we created the Singapore Institute of Technology. And in the SIT, there are various specialisation fields where, after education in polytechnic or ITE, you can join as a university programme to deepen your skills. In fact that is not enough. After SIT, we will have SkillsFuture, we will have lifelong learning, to continue to deepen the skills. And that is how we become excellent, and how we will have mastery, and the economy can become competitive.

Chairperson: Thank you, Minister. I think we have actually run out of time. But before I end, I would like to give the panel 30 seconds each, to just perhaps say the most important thing they think about inclusiveness.

YLK: Thanks. I have said all I have to say already about the six areas and we talked about the three important areas about healthcare, housing and public transport. Minister has spoken very eloquently about education, and the only area that we seem to have a difference from the rest is welfare. I would just like to spend one minute to talk about welfare. By adequate welfare, I am not talking about a full-blown Western welfare system. I am talking about taking care of the underprivileged and poor among us whom we at this present moment sadly do not. I am talking about people living in absolute poverty, I am talking about people who are earning less than S$500, and whose kids forgo meals or they forgo meals so that their kids can have meals, whose kids bring water home from school in case utilities are cut off. And these problems have not gone away. And these problems can be quite easily and affordably solved if, for example, we raise the Welfare Income Supplement (WIS) from the currently measly average S$150 a month largely in CPF to, let's say, S$400–S$600 a month largely in cash. I am talking about looking after our elderly poor, who have worked all their lives for us, built this nation from their sweat and tears, who now find themselves retiring without adequate retirement funding. I am talking about people whom we already have this scheme called the Silver Support Scheme, which we are paying a measly S$200 a month. If we raise it to S$500-S$600 a month, they would be measurably better off, they would be above decent level of living. That's what I'm talking about. The grand total of this will come up to something like 0.7–0.8% of GDP, something we can well afford. So again as we cover housing, healthcare and public transport, yes we can. And I am not talking just about progress in terms of a tax-light system, I am talking about progress as sufficient social spending on average. I am not talking about excess. Yes we can. So my question is: Why don't we?

CHB: I think the government has done a lot in terms of transfers and if you look at wage income growth in the last couple of years it has converged for the lower income and the middle class. I think in terms of housing costs, in terms of the supply, in terms of healthcare, Pioneer Generation, I guess for me there seems to be some disconnect between what businesses are saying in comparison with the government, because I think the noises are loudest from there. Clearly growth is struggling, manufacturing — even though we have diversified the economy — is in a recession as share of GDP has dropped from 25% to about 16%. And if we are going the way of Hong Kong, it is going to be a hollowing out. I am very concerned about the repercussions and I think there is a clear tradeoff, whether policies have shifted to the left, whether social policies have become the overarching objectives outshining the concerns of the economy such as the performance of the SMEs.

TKY: I think that there is a general sense of concern not just from Hak Bin but at the business level and other levels on Singapore's competitiveness and economic sustainability. What are our future pillars of growth? I would like to address that issue. When I was Chief Economist, every morning when I woke up, that was my main problem. But now since I am no longer Chief Economist, I can go to the treadmill rather than worry about these pillars of growth. Now, our nation-building gave us these two key values apart from the others as we pointed out earlier. Plurality — we are a multiracial, multicultural and multi-religious society. The second key pillar is meritocracy. It has served our political nation-building well. But I would like to argue that it would serve our future economic growth competitiveness and sustainability very well over the next 10 to 20 years. Why am I optimistic about this? Well, partly because every morning when I wake up I still think about the sustainability. Asia, as you are aware, is a very dynamic region now. It is also a very diverse region; there are a lot of geopolitical rivalries. Within the region, you have players like India, China, Japan and ASEAN. And outside the region, you have players like the US and Europe that are coming in. Now, even though we don't have a huge market, big demographic dividend, etc. — we are relatively small, if we sustain our hub city status, we will be alright. If you look around the whole region, there are a lot of monocultural regional centres. Tokyo is one, Shanghai is one. Hong

Kong is increasingly becoming one. That means within the Asia-Pacific region, Singapore is the only pluralistic hub where we are able to absorb all the other players and they are comfortable here. And more significantly, the monocultural city hubs are becoming more nationalistic, which gives us another opportunity. That means if we sustain ourselves, we can have a competitive advantage as a major hub city, where all the major players who are either within the region or outside the region feel comfortable, and that will allow us to sustain our hub city for finance, business services, logistic centre, art and culture, air and sea hub, etc. And that will be our loco-motive, and all the not so efficient SMEs can be pulled along as a wagon and we should be alright.

OYK: I will make three short points. First, I think having a light progressive tax system and all kinds of social programmes (education, preschool, fresh-start system, workfare system) that encourage even the lower-income to work and get a negative income tax benefit.... All these, when you take it one by one, maybe the impact is not as big, but when you combine them all, they are a holistic social uplifting system that the government has done. And I think it has produced good results although we are not done yet. Second, on Lam Keong's point, which is that there is so much more that he wants to do, and of course we are not done yet and we will continue to see how we can encourage and continue to bring about inclusive growth. But really "yes we can", it is a very good campaign slogan, and someone has won before using that. But when you hit the ground to implement, we also need to ask how, at what cost, who has to pay, and in the long term what is the impact? So I think it is not as straightforward. But having said that, this is the direction, as everyone can see in the last 10 years, the government has been moving towards. And so my last point is to thank everyone.

This discussion is less controversial than I expected. And maybe it is really because of the 10 years of effort, of watching our growth and at the same time ensuring that the mass benefits. Therefore, we have more or less coalesced around as a country on positions that we decide "maybe this is where we are going." But I hear Hak Bin and Kong Yam loud and clear too, that there has to be growth. I also agree with that. I think that gradually we are bringing everyone together, that we must have a common agenda. There will always be more left policies, more right policies. These will always need to be surfaced and they will always need to be debated. So thank you very much for this very interesting session.

The Future of "We"

Chairperson:
Debra Soon, Head of the Family and Premier Segment, MediaCorp TV Pte Ltd

Speaker:
Heng Swee Keat (HSK), Minister for Finance

Panel:
Ho Kwon Ping (HKP), Chairman of the Board of Trustees, Singapore Management University

Bilahari Kausikan (BK), 2015/16 S R Nathan Fellow for the Study of Singapore

Chan Heng Chee (CHC), Chairman of the Lee Kuan Yew Centre for Innovative Cities, Singapore University of Technology and Design

Chairperson: Good afternoon, everyone. Thank you very much for the introduction. Our topic today is for the final conference session, "The Future of 'We'". It is a rather philosophical question and I shall not claim any expertise in the area, as you are here also to listen to our distinguished panel of guests. So it is my duty instead to introduce them well, and as you already have their bios in the book, I am going to try something slightly different and to introduce them in the context of how I first met them.

First of all, Minister Heng Swee Keat, most of you will know or well remember by now, that Mr Lee Kuan Yew had said that Mr Heng was his best Principle Private Secretary. The best he ever had. No pressure at all for those who followed in his shoes! For me I remember the first time I met

Mr Heng was 20 years ago, over 20 years ago, when I interviewed him for his promotion exercise when he was still in the Singapore Police Force. He might not remember this. At the time he was highlighted as one of the highfliers to be featured. What struck me about him then, and I am sure is still true today, was his humility, his commitment to public service, and him thanking the men and women who worked for him to help him get to where he was.

Fast forward to today, as Finance Minister, it can be argued that Mr Heng is clearly the most experienced member in the fourth-generation leadership team — having been brought into politics only in 2011 and leading the Education Ministry soon after, before handing over to two acting ministers after the most recent general election. Now of course Mr Heng's abilities can be inferred by the tasks he has been given, including chairing Our Singapore Conversation and the SG50 Committee before the general elections. And now more importantly the Committee on Future Economy, which in the President's Address on Friday, quoting President Tony Tan, "*will* develop the strategy is to *ensure* that Singapore remains relevant and competitive." Emphasis purely mine. Tall order, but it is clear that the Prime Minister and the Cabinet has confidence in Mr Heng's abilities.

As for the rest of our distinguished panel, in alphabetical order, Ambassador Bilahari Kausikan, most of you will know him for his long career in the foreign service. He retired in 2013 as Permanent Secretary of the Ministry. He is well known for his intellect and his insightful analysis of geopolitics. Those of you who are active on Facebook will also realise, even though he was not an early adopter, he has become quite swiftly an expert with the platform. I am sure that you will agree that he never minces his words and his views are always worth sharing, even if you do not agree with them.

He has also been known to be a very colourful character with associated colourful vocabulary. My first encounter with him was when he had a short stint as the spokesperson of the Foreign Affairs Ministry, and was Press Secretary to the Minister, when I had an earful of that colourful language. One appreciates his candour in person and perhaps even better from a distance when reading his writing.

Next, Ambassador Chan Heng Chee, who needs no introduction, having had a stellar career as an academic and a diplomat. She has been a trailblazer, not just for Singapore women, but for all Singaporeans. Many of us will remember her as the longest-serving ambassador to the United States, and for the crucial role she played for improving bilateral ties between Singapore and the US. My first encounter with Professor Chan was when she was Chairman of the Singapore International Foundation, again, quite a while ago. She will probably also not remember me from then but I definitely do remember her. It was her ability to project her intellect, ask the most intelligent question in the room, and make the most sensible remarks, and project the uniqueness and specialness of Singapore and Singaporeans in one package, which struck and inspired me, and I am sure, many other Singaporean women. These qualities have helped Singapore and Singapore women punch above their weight internationally.

Last but not least, Mr Ho Kwon Ping, Chairman of Banyan Tree Holdings and Chairman of the Singapore Management University. Distinguished corporate leader, Mr Ho was also the first person to be awarded the S R Nathan Fellowship for the Study of Singapore by Institute of Policy Studies (IPS). He held a series of five lectures on economy and business, politics, governance, society, identity, security, sustainability and so on, which till today many people talk about. Some people mentioned them earlier. Mr Ho is also a newsmaker so I have had occasion to meet him at several events. But most of my interaction with him was when he was Chairman of MediaCorp, which is why I am treading very carefully. He was always very concerned about journalists and journalism, then and now, because I infer that at the very core of it, he cares about Singapore and the country's future, and believes we should have frank conversations about politics and our future, not only behind closed doors but in public.

I am more than privileged to be on this distinguished panel and hope to facilitate a free-flowing, interesting debate amongst them before turning the floor open to you for questions. But first without further ado, can I invite Mr Heng to share a few words with us.

HSK: You know, as Debra made the introduction I sank deeper and deeper into my chair with the weight of expectation that she is putting on me.

Thank you all for staying back for this session, even though I know this is the last session. You have already heard three of my colleagues, and I understand you have had very interesting sessions earlier on with [Ong] Ye Kung, [Ng] Chee Meng, and [Chan] Chun Seng earlier this morning.

You know, when I was a student, if there was a session in the afternoon and I had already had two sessions in the morning, I'd usually skip the session. And the fact that all of you stayed here, I think that there are only three possible reasons. One, it's really that somehow there's an innate quality in you that wants to endure hardship and pain. Second, after hearing Debra's introduction of our three eminent panellists, I think there is a very good reason for you to stay back, and I truly believe in teamwork. So if you have good questions please ask our panellists as well. And the third possible reason is that — I recently met a businessman and he said "I think the economy is okay because you are still smiling." So at which point I smiled a bit more and said, "Please take care of your business."

Now I think it is very interesting that the session is titled "The Future of 'We'". It could have been, "Do we have a future?" But instead the session is really about "The Future of 'We'". And I think that by itself is significant. That we are not talking about whether we have a future, but really what kind of future and how do we build that future. And since we are talking about the future — really the future is about change.

Let me make a few brief remarks about change — what I think will not change and what I think will almost definitely change. But first what will not change. I think the facts of our existence will not change. The fact that we are a small country, with no natural resources except our people. That you are in a region that can be volatile. That you have to abide by global forces, which you have a limited ability to shape. And I think that those are things which probably [Chan] Heng Chee and Bilahari [Kausikan] would agree with me.

And the other aspect, which is probably less obvious but equally impor- tant is, I would say, that as we saw in the SG50 celebration — which is I hope that the spirit and values of our people — that quality of resource- fulness and resilience and responsibility, I hope that that will not change.

In 50 years, over the next 50 years, I think the basic facts of our existence will not change. In the US, whether Detroit goes down and Palo Alto comes up really doesn't matter for the US as a country. It means some hardship for the people but [for] the US as a whole, it doesn't really matter. For us, whether Singapore stays where it is or whether things happen elsewhere mean survival for us. And you have that one city and one city state and that is that. And I think that fact will not change. So, this need to have an outward orientation, to think long term, and all that, I believe that that should not change.

Now what will change? Let me use the first letter of all my panellists' names to help me remember all these things that I think will change. And first starting with Heng Chee. Heng Chee starts with "H" and I think the word that comes close to mind is really about "hopes". And I think hopes will change. The hopes and aspirations of our people will change.

During the pioneer generation events that were held, what I found very interesting was that in the pioneer generation, when you asked them to "describe life when you started," they all say, "Well, you know, it was a very simple goal. It's a matter of survival. You don't even think too hard about it, just do it, go and get things done. And [be] happy that we have food on the table." And I remember one lady who came to the Tampines tribute event for Mr Lee, and she described how her parents used to be *chee cheong fun* sellers in the Kreta Ayer area, and how during the Communist... during those early days of riots that were inspired by the Communist United Front, her parents' chee cheong fun sauce, which had been carefully prepared overnight for many, many hours would just be overturned. And she said "For my parents, the hopes and dreams were very simple. We just wanted to survive to be able to bring up our kids. I will do whatever it takes. They were totally uneducated but they were the most well informed about what they need and what they need to do."

But when I interact with our young participants in Our Singapore Conversation, and when I went to schools, universities, and talked to our students today, it's a completely different set of hopes and dreams. They have ideas about careers that I've not even heard of. They want to live a life of purpose, they want to make a difference. A job is not just about earning an income, it is more than that. It is really about "How do I make a difference? How do I lead a meaningful life?" And I think it is a good change, it just shows how much our hopes and dreams have changed.

And similarly our seniors are very different. We are going to have 900,000 seniors by 2030. And that, I think, will be a generation that is very different and will change. I recently watched a programme on Channel NewsAsia on the hip-hop grannies in China. And it was really fascinating to see these grannies doing hip-hop with their teenagers. So while I can't quite imagine Heng Chee doing hip-hop — but certainly she can do a lot of mental hip-hops, I mean, can you imagine, it is a very different set of hopes and aspirations even for people in their different age. So hopes and dreams will change.

Second, if I turn to Bilahari, Bilahari has been spending all his life protecting our borders and building bridges across borders, and is now called Ambassador-at-Large. I don't know whether it's because we can't find him or whether he's going all over the place.

Chairperson: Larger than life maybe.

HSK: If you look at national borders, how it has changed, even for terrorism, when we talk about the Wilayah that ISIS is seeking to establish, it is truly across borders. If you look at how ICT has completely changed our notion of what it means to be a national business. You look at e-commerce, during last year's 11/11 sales by Alibaba, Singapore was ranked fifth highest in the Alibaba sales. Billions of dollars of sales. If you were operating a retail store you would not expect that a Chinese company, you would not expect 10 years ago that a Chinese company called Alibaba would be cannibalising your business. And so how ICT is really changed the borders.

Two days ago I was in Beijing for the Asian Infrastructure Investment Bank (AIIB), the establishment of the AIIB. Ministers and senior officials from 57 countries attended that event. One minister pulled me aside and said "Wow, what a change. In just a few years China has the power to command these 57 members, including some of the biggest countries in Europe, Central Asia, and Asia, even Africa, and Latin America." And when you think about it, it was significant that he made that remark about change and how during the Asian Financial Crisis, I was in the Prime Minister's Office, and we were talking about how China was making this transition and all the difficulties that it went through. And now China is saying that "I'm going to put money on the table, we are going to set up AIIB, and the rest of you please join us and let's work to develop the region."

So borders, whether it is across the world, across business, or even across disciplines in our study, will change. And that change, I think, will have a profound effect on what we do.

Now the third area of change, and now I will turn to Kwon Ping. Kwon Ping starts with "K" and I think "K" reminds me of "kinship". And Kwon Ping has also done a lot of work in SMU, trying to not only develop a sense of kinship in SMU but also getting SMU students to do social work, to do community projects — to really make them feel that they are part of Singapore, that they have to contribute to the well-being of other people.

Now I think that our societies will become more diverse and the affiliation and the sense of identity will also change. I think you are going to have Singaporeans with multiple affiliations and so on. But when you look back at our founding ideals and why we became an independent nation to begin with, it's that the sense of identity, the sense that regardless of race, language or religion, it is a really critical part of our founding ideals. When you think about that colonial struggle and what happened, the people at that period of time had basically a few options. Either go back to the countries that they came from or seek to develop a different society in Southeast Asia. And Mr Lee and his team decided that they would try to build a multi-racial nation out of the rural groups of people, immigrants coming from different parts of the world. And I would say that over 50 years the sense that regardless of race, language, or religion, it's now quite well embedded in our society. But it is always a work in progress it is something that we must never forget. And indeed we will find new sources of differences, be it socio-economic status, be it wealth, be it beliefs, be it interests and so on.

And really it's not so much a change per se, but it is my hope that this sense of kinship will remain strong in our society.

And finally, Debra starts with "D", and Debra is always associated with dialogue and debates and so on, I will turn to Debra and say, really it's more about "dialogue".

I tell you that I personally, between debates and dialogue, I far prefer dialogue. Because I think that you can get deep into an issue, you can surface assumptions that we have, we can go deep into a conversation and try to reach something positive. And I would say that we must go even beyond that. That it is not just about talking, it is about how we can agree on certain actions, how we can then work together to achieve what we hope to do.

So those are the four changes, and if you think about it, essentially when we talk about how hopes will change, it is really an internal wish list. That each of us has our hopes, has our dreams, has our aspirations, and our hopes will change.

We talk about borders, it is really about what happens outside us, what happens around the world, and how global forces will continue to shape our small little island-state.

And when we talk about kinship, it is really the glue that binds, that gives us a sense that we are one people, that we need to have this sense of togetherness, and to have this sense of care and concern for one another that will enable us to build a better society, to build a better future together. That we are in this together.

And finally it is not just each of us expressing our wishes and dreams, but it is how feeling that sense of kinship that we can come together to do things together, to develop deeper understanding and trust with one another. To see how, for example, the things that we do in Our Singapore Conversation, in SG50, and now in "The Future of Us" exhibition, can allow us to achieve that common understanding and that collective will to do things together.

So when we talk about "The Future of 'We'" I think the future really, at the end of the day, is for us to shape. Not just by one or two persons, but really by all of us together. It is a collective endeavour. And I will stop there. Thank you.

Chairperson: Thank you very much, Minister. Could I just ask the first question, that when you talk about race, language and religion, and change — and that these are core principles which should not change, do we not acknowledge that there are global forces, particularly on religion, on the front of conservatism across the globe which have already affected us here, how do we deal with these forces of change, how will they affect us as we try to develop kinship?

Perhaps you first and then I will open up to the panellists.

HSK: Well, I think that there will always be differences in our society. What I think is very important is that when it comes to matters of religion it is not possible for... it is not something that you can empirically falsify. Unlike a scientific hypothesis, where you can say, "Well this is correct and this is wrong because I can prove it, you can't." This is the nature of faith. I don't think therefore when it comes to dialogue that it would be productive for us to say, "Let us debate whether your God is truer than my God." I don't think that is possible. But what is possible is to make sure that we find as much common points of reference as possible, and that we create platforms for different religious groups to come together to work on things that they can agree on and develop a degree of trust. So that is the first thing.

Second, many people will agree that sometimes religions can be subverted for other purposes and it is important that we are vigilant towards that. And those believers who feel that their religion has been subverted — that you have a more extreme form that does not respect other religions, that does not give space to other religions — that's something that people of that faith will have to act on and to make sure that it does not become a source of conflict. Because it will certainly bring conflicts, and it will bring a range of issues that will be very hard to deal with once it unravels.

Chairperson: Prof. Chan, may I asked you to jump in there please?

CHC: Thank you, Debra. Race, language, religion. These are primeval forces. And I would say that the history of Singapore, from colonial times till now, has been really about trying to manage race, language, and religion, and the development of a multi-racial, multi-lingual, multi-religious, multi-cultural policy. I think we have done reasonably well so far. We can say we live in racial harmony, we can say, you know, there is racial peace, far more than you see what's happening in Baltimore, Ferguson; it's a very different picture now.

We had 9/11 in Singapore and we discovered the Jemaah Islamiya (JI) network. And yet, in spite of that, I think the Muslim community does not feel targeted the way they are elsewhere. And we have worked hard at it. And keeping this harmony still requires work. I think we cannot say that we've got it, we've reached a stage of integration, we're getting on reasonably well. Because if you don't keep managing and working at these issues, things can fall apart.

Chairperson: Well actually the context of my question was because recently the religious right have been protesting against, for instance, the inclusion of Adam Lambert in the countdown party. And in addition to that, I think the MDA [Media Development Authority] is dealing with the issue of Madonna's concert in Singapore, and that religious conservatism has kind of narrowed the common space we have here. Would Mr Ho like to jump in?

HKP: Could I actually bring up a different topic instead?

Chairperson: Sure.

HKP: When we discussed the future of Singapore, I think there is a general agreement that whatever that future is going to be it is going to have to involve an increasingly active civil society. I think that everyone is well aware of [that].

And one of the things that I encountered during my time having to be the S R Nathan lecturer is that I try to speak to many people in civil society, and of course people had many different views, very different views. But one common view that came about, and it's something that I would like to ask Minister… incidentally, just to make sure that there is no added pressure to you, sir, many people have said that this is a beauty parade of future prime ministers and Mr Heng appears to be the front runner. No pressure, sir, no pressure. And if this were America we would be asking each one of the speakers today, "What is it you are going to do that differentiates you from your competitor and your predecessor?" But we are in Singapore, we are very united, we all speak with one tongue.

But nevertheless, sir, I think I've been asked to ask you something quite specific. And I think it's an issue that is quite burning for many members of civil society, whether it be academia or lobby groups, whether it be animal rights groups or whatever. And the concern that they seem to have, regardless of their perspective, is this whole issue of information access. You are well aware of that and it has been spoken about by other people.

Complaints are being made that we are not even talking about confidential information or restricted information, but general access to information from the bureaucracy, the civil service, and so on. And it has been proposed that having a Freedom of Information Act is too radical for Singapore. But one proposal was that other countries seem to have a code of conduct for government civil servants, a code of conduct whereby, essentially it sets out as a code of conduct, not as a legal document as much as a Freedom of Information Act, but a code of conduct whereby — except for specific circumstances regarding security and so on — all information should be made easily available to the public.

And the sense I got from many groups I spoke to was that they feel that information is the lifeblood of dialogue and of civil society. So the question I pose to you, sir, is what would you do as a future prime minister about information access? Would you approve of such a bill sir?

HSK: Your question is so hypothetical I don't think I have to answer it now. But in the spirit of answering the essence of your question... not the implication of the question.

First, on your point of civil society's interest in doing their part for Singapore. In fact, one of the things I have said on many occasions is that, really, as our society becomes more diverse and as our people become [better] educated, it is an opportunity for us to harness that energy and creativity of all Singaporeans to build a better Singapore. It is not possible for government agencies to do everything, to know everything. Nor do we have the monopoly of all the good ideas. And one of the things... so for instance on the Committee of the Future Economy, one of the things that I intend to do is to consult as widely as possible to get as many points of view as possible. At the end of it of course we then have to debate the pros and cons, there will be groups that will be opposing A versus B and so on. And some groups will be winners and some groups will be losers, and government as the arbitrator will have to think about what we have to do for the long-term, for the good of all our people.

So I think that there are lots of avenues for people to participate in meaningful dialogues. I recently received a report from the Singapore Business Federation (SBF); the SBF has, on its own initiative, in fact more than six months ago gotten all its members together and put out an excellent report, very thoughtful report, on what we need to do. And as I said before, I was most impressed with the fact that although businesses have to worry about quarterly results and short-term and so on, more than two-thirds of the recommendations were about the medium-term and long-term. And I think that this is a quality of involvement, which I hope that we will get. That people are not just looking at "what is in it for me, for my business," but really what is… how can we collaborate, enlarge the pie, and take care not just of today but tomorrow. And I think that this is something to be very much encouraged.

When I did Our Singapore Conversation (OSC) I structured it in such a way that it was completely open-ended. In fact my colleagues were quite shocked at that. "Are you sure that you can conduct a dialogue where you just ask Singaporeans to come together and talk about their aspirations? And their hopes and dreams for the future?" And I said well you have to start from there, because I don't want to set up first a subcommittee on ABCDE, and then to direct the dialogue in a particular direction. I really want to hear from fellow Singaporeans what matters to you the most. And what was most encouraging out of this OSC was how many points of convergence there were and I think we need to have that confidence that Singaporeans are thoughtful, reasonable people and that we should engage as deeply as possible.

What came out of it too was that a lot of them came up to me and said, "Gee, I didn't realise that other people have perspectives that are so different from mine." So from that point of view I believe that civil society in Singapore, while they are set up for particular causes or to advocate particular causes or they have particular areas of interest, should always do this, not so much with a view of just narrowly advocating a particular set of interest. Even if you are interested in animal rights, one needs to consider the interests of people who may have issues with safety and so on. And so it is really that balance we need in our society and I am quite confident that as we are more engaged in the process of dialogue, we will deepen that understanding within our society and across the different parts of our society.

And now specifically about your point about information being… whether it should be made more readily available, I can confess to you that even as Finance Minister I don't get all the information I want. I sometimes ask, "How come I don't get the analysis on this?" And either the information is not collected or some departments say "but this is not relevant to the Ministry of Finance." And I do think that as a society we need to be better at using data, we need to be better at looking at how we can have more data-driven policymaking and data-driven work.

But having said that this has been raised from time to time, when I look at... I don't know how many of you have seen the Department of Statistics website. It's a whole range of interesting information that one could make fairly good use of, even just whatever is available. So as we embark on the Smart Nation project, as we look at... not only will the amount of data that government will be collecting and putting out be increasing, but actually many private sector players are putting out lots of those data.

SMU, for instance, you have a data analytics project. And those are data that no one has ever collected and which SMU will be doing, with regard to the confidentiality of individuals and so on, which will give us very interesting results. So I think that if our question is how do we be more data-driven in our policymaking, in the way that we think about issues, in the way we run businesses and so on, I would say that certainly the government will be providing more in those areas in the coming years. But also I think it's not just about government, it's also about what the private sector can do, and what we can do to make use of those data.

Chairperson: Bilahari, would you like to jump in there, do you think we need a Freedom of Information Act, and whether or not we should be revealing all to the public and to civil society?

BK: Let me go back to your first point of entry about race, language and religion.

I agree with Heng Chee; these are primordial things; they are never going to go away entirely. They will morph but they will always be there. And one of the rules for dealing with it in a multi-racial society is: You need a state that is strong enough to be a neutral arbiter among different races, different religions, different confessions. That is absolutely vital.

But the problem in much of the world is that the state is too weak or the state has handicapped itself, especially in the so-called first world. I think that, by the way, as an aside, we should get rid of this narrative, "From Third World to First". We know we have gone there, but that is no longer a good benchmark for the next phase because if you look at the first world, many of them are extremely dysfunctional.

So the point is not to be mired in the same problems. And one of the problems that you see in Europe, they are unable, incapable, of dealing with extremism — extremism in religion — not because the state is a failed state, because they are all functional states, but they have handicapped themselves by their own ideologies. Now that is perhaps related not so much to Freedom of Information, but to a broader question which I was going to ask the Minister, but I ask it now anyway.

You know, when you talked about what will not change.

HSK: What will *not* change?

BK: What will not change. And I agree with you, absolutely, how can I not agree with you? Because I spent most of my life dealing with that right? But you know Minister, I hope you know, that a substantial amount of the population is not going to believe you. I do not mean people in this room — I hope I don't mean people in this room! But your broader audience, many of them, a substantial amount, I mean there is no way to quantify it but I believe so, are going to see this as just another ploy to keep the PAP government in power.

And so when the President, in his address, spoke about the need for good politics, the need to refresh our system, to continue to have good politics, the question arises "what is good?" What is the benchmark? And I don't think the first world necessarily provides all the benchmarks. I think we will have to chart our own course and I would like to know, what is your vision for that course? Thank you. A simple question.

HSK: Thank you, Bilahari, for that question. First of all, I can't agree with you more that our benchmark, especially when it comes to managing social, even economic and political issues should not be the so-called "first world". It's not as if that there was that gold standard that we must all strive towards.

I've always believed that every society must decide for itself — what is it that it wants, what are the challenges that it faces, what are the circum-stances in which they are in. And then have the courage and conviction to figure out how [to] get there. And of course a very critical element of it is to have a population who believes that this is the way to go. So if we take that approach — that is why I mentioned what is it that will change and what will not change; and the reason why I outlined what are the things that will not change, the circumstances that we are faced with and so on — and the examples that I gave of how, if you look at 10 years ago, 15 years ago, people will not be talking about China convening an Asia Infrastructure and Investment Bank (AIIB) and so on.

In fact, during the Asian Financial Crisis we were saying, "Oh dear what would happen to China?" and so on. So things changed very quickly and we have to figure out for ourselves what is it that we need to do and do differently; because you are in this part of Asia, you face a set of imperatives within this region and if we blindly adopt methods used elsewhere we are going to be in trouble. And the circumstances will always change and you have to find new ways of doing things.

In preparing for my budget, I read one of Dr Goh's [Goh Keng Swee] earlier budget speech. That was way back in 1967. And it was a fascinating speech because I wanted to understand what were the circumstances that we were faced with then — what did we do and how did we get out of it. Not because there are specifics of policy that will be helpful today, but rather I wanted to claim the spirit of that problem-solving. What was it that was done?

And it is interesting that Kwon Ping asked about data. There was actually a lot of very good data that was produced, that was sufficient for us to analyse what the problems were and what we needed to do. So I think that we need to really figure out what other changes are going to happen around us.

Now unfortunately, and I agree, Bilahari, that sometimes people get very cynical and say, "Here again Mr Heng is talking about all these vulnerabilities and smallness and so on." So let me say two things about that point.

First of all, I think we will be very unwise to ignore that these are facts that we have to confront. And however difficult it is to get the message across, I think it is part of our responsibility in the leadership, and in fact all of you here, to go out and talk about this. Because these are things that empirically you could either say, "This is all a whole load of rubbish" or you can come up with fairly reasoned analysis and say "Indeed, those are the

103

facts of life." And I believe that, if you talk to business people, they will understand what it is. We have a good tripartite system. I believe that our workers will understand what is it we need to do. In fact, the unions have actually brought some of our workers around the world including China, to see the enormous changes that have taken place.

And the second reason why I think we need to talk about that is that: It is not just to focus our mind on the fact that we are small, the fact that we do not have natural resources and all that. In fact, I mention it for opposite reasons. That we should really think hard about how to turn the fact of smallness to unique value and relevance to the world. How do we turn the fact we are without natural resources to build a unique advantage? I think all of you are familiar with the water story and how we overcame the constraints. I believe that we are going to be able to make an impact in education, in how we educate our young people, in how our universities are structured, how our poly[technics] and ITE and now SkillsFuture are structured because when we recognise a problem and not deny it, we can be innovative, we can be creative about things, we can do far more than if we pretend that the problem does not exist.

Similarly, the fact of our smallness can be turned into an advantage even in foreign affairs. Why is the Shangri-La Dialogue held in Singapore? Where major powers convene here? Because we are small and we are non-threatening, and therefore we can play a nice neutral role. Yesterday I hosted 21 Nobel laureates and technology prizewinners at Singapore University of Technology and Design (SUTD). I asked them "What made you come to Singapore? We are a very small place and to have this team of very eminent scientist?" And they said "Well, precisely because you are small you have to do things quite differently and this is one of those few conferences where you bring people from different disciplines together across borders, across boundaries of discipline. And we find it very stimulating."

And therefore I think by recognising where we are and what the constraints are, we are in a better position to transcend [them] and to do something really creative about it.

Now on your question about "What is good politics? How would I regard it?" Let me share that recently we had a discussion amongst a whole group of ministers about a major infrastructure project, and the major infrastructure project is divided into many different phases. The first phase will not come on until at least 15 years from now and the last part of it, if we want to have the option to do better, will not take place until another 30–40 years from now. I had taken part in the discussion in a very matter-of-fact way, "Oh this is what we should be thinking about" and so on. Until a colleague of mine, a public servant who was involved in the discussion said, "This is surreal, you know? If you don't mind me saying, none of you are going to be alive! And here you are talking about this. Don't you understand that a week in politics is a long time? And here you are talking about projects for Singapore over this long period of time. And none of you will be alive!"

And that's where it hit me. I said "yes, indeed." I took it as a matter of course that we are in it to protect, to advance the long-term interests of Singapore. To think about the generations of Singaporeans, those who are here with us and those who are not even born yet. And I believe strongly that that ought to be an instinct.

Second, I think that the other instinct [is that] we need to really understand the world and what are the changes that are happening around us if we are going to help to navigate this small place.

And third, as I said in my remarks, as our society becomes better educated and more diverse, we have a lot more knowledge and expertise, and energy and creativity out there. And we've got to find better ways in which we can harness that energy and creativity of our people to do great things together. But that starts from the dialogue, from having a common understanding and that is why I have been so passionate about the Singapore conversation — and about the "Future of Us" exhibition and about the way we are going to do the Committee on the Future Economy. Because I think it would be dumb, right, if I were to say, "This is what I know and this is how I will decide and that's that." Because at the end of the day all these changes that we have to make in our society, whether it is a big macro policy, or whether it is about how you develop the community, has to come from our people.

And I am very happy that as an MP on the ground, over the last four-and-a-half, five years, I have met so many groups of residents that come together to do really interesting things together. It need not be very highbrow stuff, and great debates of policy and politics and all that; it could just be really simple things. I share with you one that I am so impressed

[with]. A group of my residents came together and said, "You know, we have quite a number of aged people in our area and we have all these void decks in this area, these lovely void decks. Can we use this to set up a neighbour's corner?" And I said "Yeah, why not?" "So can you support us?" I said "What do you need?" "Well, just give us the space and we need some basic facilities, give us some small amount of raw materials for us to cook." I said, "Well, that sounds easy enough."

And then someone else came and volunteered and said, "Oh, I am happy to donate a TV," "I'm happy to do this," "I'm happy to donate tables and chairs," and "I'm happy to do that." And today there is a whole group of elderly, from their late 60s to 70s and some in their 80s, who will come together to cook for one another. They have breakfast there every day. There was a great spirit of neighbourliness. And those are the things that we should all promote. So I'm saying that the range of participation in what we do is really, really very wide and diverse. And that the needs in our society will grow, and that sort of energy, and care and concern for others is really what we must continue to promote.

So on the one level we need to make sure that internationally, whether it is in foreign policy, whether it is in our defence, whether it is in our economic policy, that we are able to keep pace with the world. And on another level, that what we do internally, that you have to build that sense of togetherness and that can be done through a whole variety of interesting ways. It doesn't have to be just in one or two specific areas.

Chairperson: Thank You Minister. We have time for one more question from the panel, would any of you like to jump in? Prof. Chan?

CHC: Since it takes a long time to come back to the beginning, I will ask two questions at the same time. They have to do with political changes. Now the title of this session is "The Future of 'We'". And "we" implies subject, active. As opposed to the future of "us", which is the object. Things happened to "us". Things are done to "us". Things are done for "us" — but "we" will do this.

You are going to have a much more active citizenry, Minister. We talked about the role of Civil Service Organisations (CSOs). I think the question I have here is: Will there be a change, a re-examination of political style going forward for the next 50 years? Not the last 50 years. That things will be less top-down, leadership will be less top-down, but the government will let things float from bottom — white space allowing citizens to decide what they want to do and really full engagement civil society? That is the first question.

The second question has to do with the titillating speech during the opening of Parliament by the President. He spoke of political changes to the political system. And so I asked myself what changes are we thinking of? Is it to the constituencies, to the GRCs? Is it to the elected presidency? And I think today Kishore Mahbubani had an article on the elected presidency. So are we thinking of anything along those lines? I must confess I was never a fan of the elected presidency because it really confuses the electorate. We are a prime ministerial system, and we grafted the elected system. And some of the candidates of the last elected presidential election thought they were going to be fully empowered. But it is not. This is a prime ministerial system with Cabinet responsibility. So that is very confusing.

But what I think I felt the elected presidency did was that it gave less of an opportunity for the minorities to really occupy the seat of the presidency when you have a national electorate. So it is a pity that we cannot rotate to the different ethnic minorities the way we used to in the past by appointment. So my question is: The political changes, are you changing political styles substantially, and second, what is going to happen to the elected presidency?

HSK: Heng Chee, thanks for the question. First, on your first question about whether the stance will change: actually I would say that if you look at the government, the stance has been changing over the years. When I was starting my work on Our Singapore Conversation, I looked back at all the previous consultations that we did from The Next Lap to the various sessions that were done over that period of time. And you notice that in fact every few years there were some of these changes; and I think most people would agree that Mr Goh Chok Tong had a very different style from Mr Lee Kuan Yew, and PM has a very different style too.

And in fact if at all, I would say that the trend has been towards increasing openness and participation. And I believe for a very good reason. Which is that there is — as we are able to build a better common understanding of how we secure our collective interest and how do we enable our people to be able to fulfil their potential — I think the greater confidence and trust have been built up over time allows us to do a lot more of this. And I would stress that the important thing is that we start, as I mentioned earlier, not from a very narrow interest-based politics or a narrow identity based politics; because I think that will be negative for Singapore, it could even potentially be destructive.

And you look at what is happening in many systems around the world, where politics is really based on a contest of different groups. And one group setting up lobbies of one form or another, and in the end the political process does not take into account the interest of as many people as possible because it is really a function of how much money you can raise to lobby for a particular course. And I don't think that that would be good for Singapore.

Now would it be consultative across many things and so on? I would say that it really depends on the subject matter. If you are dealing with a subject on our security, on terrorism, I don't think it's something that one would say, "Let me consult before I make an arrest." I think you've just got to be very decisive about it and say that's that. That as long as there is a proper due process where there are serious infringements of the law I don't think we want that to be open to consultation and discussion.

But on the other hand if you are talking about: how do we ensure that we can better safeguard ourselves from terrorism? That is something that will benefit from a better airing of views. To build their consensus in our society, that we won't allow this to happen here. If it happens we have a way to respond, we have a way to make sure that it does not care about our social fabric. Then that would be important.

On your question about changes and your comments about the elected president. Our political institutions will have to evolve with the times. But what should not change is that we must continue to have clean, effective governments that can take Singapore forward. That we are able to have a system that is not gridlocked, that is mired in interest-based politics, that I think must continue.

But at the same time, as our population becomes more diverse, it is important that the voices of different groups of people, and the voices of the minority in particular are heard and adequately represented in our system.

So I would not want to prejudge how the discussions will go, I think that the President has mentioned that we will continue… this will be a time for us to discuss, the government will study this, and there will be discussions on this topic. And I hope that… in fact the last few days I noticed that there has been a number of interesting opinions that have been aired.

As to the question of the confusion between the President and the fact that ours is a prime ministerial system. Indeed there is the risk of that. But I do personally think that the elected presidency is an important institution for the function of stabilising our system. That you can never predict how the election results will come out and it has a role in providing a certain stability. Again, really acting in the long term interest of Singapore. The question is how do we ensure that that remains relevant and how do we minimise any potential negatives from having a system like that.

But let me add that, apart from political institutions, I think that the political culture in our country is also very important. I recently visited a country in our region as a tourist. So during that trip I took many cab rides; I had a chat with many different people including people on the street, and I said, "You know you have a very interesting set of debates in your Parliament and sometimes it gets a little unruly." I was quite astonished when someone said, "Yeah but that is our political culture. Actually it is quite entertaining." And I said, "Surely Parliament is not the place to be entertained, it is for serious debate!" And [they] say, "Well what to do? It has become like that!"

I don't think we want to get there. I think we got to maintain a certain expectation of our political leaders, of Members of Parliament. That there is a certain decorum and a certain seriousness of purpose in our Parliament. And that I think can only come from the expectations of our people. That this is the kind of political culture that we want. Similarly when we talk about whether it is NGOs, other groups; if we are the people who stand up and say, "No, I will not just narrowly advocate what is good for me, but I really think about the interest of other people" — that creates a very different political culture and its important that we guard that. And that we don't end up like, in the case of the US where the parties have become more and more polarised because of the nature of the election, the nature of the TV and all that, it's just a lot of grandstanding. And people will tell you in private that "actually I don't believe in what I just said, but I had to say because the TV is there and all that." And that I think is very dysfunctional. And I hope that we maintain a certain seriousness of purpose in our political life.

QUESTION AND ANSWER SESSION

Chairperson: Thank you very much, Minister. I would like to now open the floor to questions. There are many mics around. If you can make your way to the closest mic near you and introduce yourself, it would be very helpful.

Q1: I have a very provocative question.... My provocative question is, I know much has been said about harmony, and also thanks for the reminder by Heng Chee, that this is work in progress; so I'd like to ask this question: how many of us, how many of you still think that the Malay Muslim community is the weakest link for Singapore? There are a lot of question marks, challenges: Daesh, Islamic State (IS), developments in the world, developments in the region, in terms of race politics in our neighbouring countries. With possible challenges to us.

Do we still think of the Malay Muslims in Singapore as the weakest link? We the Muslims in Singapore and Malay Muslims in Singapore see ourselves as a source of strength for what we contribute towards the greater wellness of Singapore, the future we, and we hope this will echo, not [only] in this room but the whole of Singapore. Not only today but forever. Of course it depends on the Malay Muslims themselves, they have to show that they are indeed a strength as part of a multi-racial, multi-religious Singapore. Thank you.

Chairperson: Thank you. Very difficult question, Minister, would you like to take that?

HSK: Well thank you. I would like to share with you one session which I attended. This was an inter-religious organisation, it was a forum about religion. And what was most remarkable for me in that particular forum was that when a bishop stood up and said, "Today we spoke about extremist views and I want, as a Christian, to make clear that extremist views can affect any religion. And in fact in any of our beliefs. It is not targeted at any particular religion."

And I was so cheered by that remark. So I think in the nature of such discussion it is important indeed for us to understand that anything, any of these comments, any belief system pursued to its extreme can become subverted, can become a source of problems for others. And I think there-fore, I kept mentioning, this respect that we have for different points of view is important, and this sense of kinship that we need to have in our society. Because if you do, then you try to enlarge the common space and the understanding.

So I don't think that we should associate, you know, just as a matter of instinct that when we talk about external development and all that.... We just have to look at where the sources of problems are and how they might affect us. When we talk about global and regional development, bear in mind that, you know I mentioned about how for instance the Internet and ICT and even e-commerce, could completely disrupt our business. All our businesses in Singapore, if we don't prepare for it, can also be disrupted.

So whether it is a matter of economics, or politics, or racial relations, developments outside us can affect us, and we have got to be quite clear about how that might be transmitted. And if we understand that I think we are in a better position to guard against that.

Chairperson: Would any of you like to respond to that question? Bilahari?

BK: No. (*Laughter*)

Chairperson: Anybody else on the floor would like to ask questions?

Q2: I run a social enterprise that promotes social inclusivity of commu-nities. But basically I would like to respond to [the first questioner's] comments as well as provide feedback to the Minister with regard to engagement of minorities, in particular the Malay Muslim community.

I understand that every single month we collect different income from each and every Singaporean to help Chinese Development Assistance Council (CDAC), Sinda. But for Muslims it actually goes to the Mosque Building Fund, and slightly a little bit goes to Mendaki. So why not... we realise that the problem that we face [as] a community, that [is] perhaps classified as a weak link, unfortunately, we do not have a Malay Muslim intermediary which is similar to the concept of CDAC, Eurasian Association or Sinda. So in other words the income that we collect from the Malay Muslim community actually goes to [the] Mosque Building Fund, goes to religion, while the challenges we face are a racial challenge. So perhaps what is needed is an intermediary — help the community groups, the many Malay-Muslim Organisations (MMOs) out there to help themselves. So perhaps the channelling of this finances would then help social issues. That is the first feedback.

The second one is: Since now is SG51, I understand that last year we increased tax deductibles to institute of public characters to 300%. Perhaps we can increase at a little bit more to promote more civil activism, as well as greater community help. So those are my two comments in response.

Chairperson: Thank you for your questions. The first one on the Mosque Building Fund.

HSK: May I ask what your social enterprise does?

Q1 (cont'd): Social creatives. We do legal vandalism. Basically we rally people to come together to paint at different locations; whether it is at the Institute of Mental Health, orphanages, void decks, art galleries, and recently at Resorts World.

HSK: That is very interesting, thank you. I hope you find that to be an interesting and meaningful thing to do.

First, let me comment on your Mendaki fund and all that. In fact, the formula for this contribution was revised some months back, I don't remember the details. But let me say that in terms of helping the different groups in Singapore: it's not just the Mendaki fund. When I was Minister for Education, I raised the bursaries for students across all races quite significantly, and we had programmes for levelling up. In primary school we started at P1 and P2, and then I moved it up all the way up to P6, and all the way to secondary school. So it is not just specific pots of funds that are earmarked for particular purpose. One has to take into account the entire approach that we have, and for me, education remains very much a critical enabler of progress. We have got to make sure that nobody, that no child, is left behind because of family circumstances.

Now on your comment about SG51, whether we should have more funding for IPC and all that. I have to commend the team who did this SG50 kinship programmes. I mean they raised a large amount of funds for the care and share programme. Lots of people really put in a lot of effort, I'm sure many of you in this room have donated in one way or another to that. And what is important for us now is to make sure that we can use those funds as effectively as possible. And I do encourage that, for different groups, to come together and to look at how we can maximise the impact of those funds.

But as to your specific suggestion, that is something that has been studied in the budget. I won't say anything about the budget at this moment.

Chairperson: Any more questions from the floor? Actually Mr Heng pre-empted my question, I was going to ask what inclusive measures would you be including in this year's budget to create more kinship amongst Singaporeans?

HSK: Ah! You see that is something that is interesting! I think that it is useful in some areas to create things like that, but in other areas, [it] can actually not be the most helpful. And I do think that when we talk about the kinship spirit, I hope it goes beyond just what the government can do in financial terms, but really it is a much broader concept, which I hope everyone embraces.

CHC: Debra can we ask another question if there is no question from the floor?

Well Mr Heng, Minister, as Kwon Ping said, this is a beauty contest, and you are who you are. So let me ask you this question: What is your most optimistic scenario for Singapore in 10 years' time? And what is your not-so-optimistic scenario for Singapore in 10 years?

HSK: Well, I don't think in terms of what is the most optimistic or what is the most pessimistic, in that sense. But I do think in terms of where I hope we will be in 10 years' time. And we can talk about a whole range of things relating to, you know, the economy, and our position in the world and so on. But I would say that at the end of the day what matters most to me is our people. And the relationships among our people.

So let me first talk about our people. I think I would like to see Singaporeans having, as I said earlier on, this sense of kinship, having that sense of care and concern for one another. Having that self-confidence to make breakthroughs, having that spirit to have that entrepreneurial spirit, that innovative spirit to take whatever that may come our way. Because we can't predict how the world will be. We can manage ourselves. We can develop that steel in us, we can develop that quality in us that says, "Whatever it is, we will stick together and we will figure out our way out." And that this care and concern that cuts across language, race, religion, will be part of the Singapore DNA. And I think if we have that spirit in us we can do many things together, we can achieve many things together. And I cannot predict what we can do together because if we are truly creative about it, many of the things that we do will surprise us.

Like for instance when we embarked on the R&D efforts, we don't expect what will happen, we were unable to predict that in a certain number of years this is what would happen. But that was what happened. When we embarked on expanding our universities, we now produce those who are a lot more knowledgeable about the world, who are able to solve a lot more problems, who are travelling the world. And I think if we focus on people we will not go very wrong.

Now the other aspect of it is really the quality of the relationship of our people. I have always been very troubled when I look around the world, how societies don't fulfil their potential or the potential of their people. Either they are spending all their time fighting issues, whether it is sectarian issue or whether it is political gridlock and so on. And the people who suffer are the common man, the man in the street. And I find that troubling. And I hope that we don't get there. And also you find that in many societies, over a period of time, groups form. And you end up with all sorts of groups, which then become very entrenched, and they want to fight for their interest.

But if we are able to structure our society in a way that allows groups to interact, to mingle, to support one another, to do meaningful things together, we will be in a far better position to fulfil our potential as a society, and will be far better able to give opportunities to our people to fulfil their aspirations. So I made a speech recently about companies. Companies are one entity that organises our people. And I said that, really at the end of the day, companies call their people "human resources", but people really go beyond a human resource. That people are at the heart of what we do, and indeed they are the source of the energy and creativity of your company. That's why when we started the Earn and Learn Programme, I felt very passionately that beyond school, companies and bosses must take an interest in developing the people who are with them, who have thrown their lot in with them.

So if we can do that, we can do a lot more things together. So those are the two things which I would say. And then you have all kinds of interesting, creative surprises.

HKP: Minister, now that Heng Chee has opened the way for us to be more provocative, can I be intentionally provocative and ask you a question which has up to now not been particularly provocative nor controversial in Singapore, but clearly it has been internationally provocative at the social level. And that is LGBT rights.

As we all know the government's position here has been one of staying away from the whole debate on the grounds that this is an issue that involves religion, that involves individual sexual orientation and preferences and so on, and it is not government's role to take a hard position. And that we need to let society evolve and government stays out of it. We also know that in the Western world, for many decades this entire issue was very controversial. Nothing really moved and you had government staying out of the fray. But we also know that in the space of less than one decade, the entire legal system changed in the Western world regarding LGBT rights. When it changed from an issue of individual preferences and social, moral, religious issues, to an issue of basic human rights. And the debate, I guess the activist that led the way to LGBT rights becoming really recognised legally, was when they changed the framework of the debate to one of human rights as opposed to individual orientation.

I guess my question is: Do you foresee that in the next 10 years this international change from which we are quite different from... how long can we stay away from it before international activists, as well as local activists, turn LGBT issues from a issue of moral, social, religious to one of basic human rights? And if that debate then becomes very vociferous in Singapore, what would you do about it? What is your position on this?

HSK: Well I think my position is not different from what we have articulated. Issues relating to values, relating to the stance that we take in particular will evolve. And if you look at how Singapore has evolved over the years there are many issues that were not discussed but now, more and more, they are being discussed. And the younger generation will be subject to a very different set of influences. There will be many different points of view. And I think what…. Let me share one of the sessions in the OSC, where this subject was actually discussed.

This was about what is the appropriate family structure. And what was interesting about that particular session was how, when participants sat down and then, face-to-face, to talk about the issue; it was not as polarising as it was, because here you have a human being in front of you talking about those issues and another human being in front of you advocating the particular issue. And I believe that that is a better way for us going forward. That essentially it is an issue that people would have to come together and said, well let us talk about what this is all about. I don't think that… I can't predict how the international trends and norms will affect us. It will certainly affect us. How quickly? I don't know. But I do hope that the way that we deal with it will not be different from the way that we deal with issues that can potentially divide us. Which is [to] have a serious dialogue over a period of time on this and then develop trust and understanding along the way, develop a better understanding of what is at stake and then let it be resolved. Rather than "this is the way of dealing with it and there is no other way."

HKP: Do you foresee a possible decriminalisation of section 377A in the next 10 years?

HSK: Well I cannot predict how things will change, but I think the stance at the moment is that we leave it as it is.

Chairperson: Yes, Bilahari?

BK: Okay, I want to ask a non-provocative question.

HKP: From you that is not possible!

Chairperson: Unusual!

BK: Just to respond to one point that Kwon Ping makes. Human rights evolve, but it does not always evolve in one direction. You can see it in Europe about the rights of refugees, but that is by the by.

I want to bring the discussion back, maybe, Minister, to this question about how we overcome the resistance that I think there is to this concept of our vulnerabilities. I agree with you, we just have to, all of us in our own way, keep plugging away as it.

HSK: Right.

BK: But one aspect of it is that I think the knowledge of where we came from. I don't think — and this is my own view, [that] we do a very good job of national education. We have an elaborate apparatus for national education but it is so ritualised that I sometimes wonder it does more harm than good. I don't think, and you were once Minister for Education, I don't think we do a particularly good job of teaching our own history to our young people. And the result is, I think, that there is a vacuum and that vacuum has been filled with a whole lot of very dodgy history. A whole lot of rubbish.

Now, do you agree with me....

HKP: That there is a whole lot of rubbish?

BK: There is a whole lot of rubbish out there? Do you agree with me that this is a problem and if so how do we solve it? I know some things are underway but by its nature, you know these things, we have probably lost a generation, you know, in terms of historical education of our own history. But we have to start rectifying it somewhere.

HKP: If that is a non-provocative question, I don't know what would be a provocative question from Bilahari.

BK: I'll tell you later!

HSK: Thanks Kwon Ping, for your kinship with me on this! And I tell you Bilahari always crosses borders when he goes at-large.

You know Bilahari I am so glad you asked that question because I have never, since I went to MOE, and after I left MOE, I have never gone to any session of discussion or even a social function when somebody didn't say, "The root cause of the problem is education."

And you have just kept my track record, so thank you very much, Bilahari!

All I can say is that I am quite happy that now I have two ministers who are my successors who are going to have to deal with this issue!

But seriously, I do think that there is a gap. There is a gap because, partly because, we have been quite reluctant to talk about history because, I know that Minister Mentor Lee Kuan Yew (MM) in particular was very uncomfortable about talking about himself. And so he wrote the book, his memoirs and all that, to help the younger people understand. But he didn't want to be seen [as] glorifying himself. And as a result of which I think the tone that was set was such that we are very reserved in the way that we teach history. And I don't think that this is a good thing.

Chairperson: You're right.

HSK: Rather unfortunately fortunately, MM's passing... that week of national mourning really created a National awakening. I had so many young people who came to the tribute event, some wrote to me, and they said, "I have never known, I've not known about all these facts of our history, and how is it that we did not teach it well in school?"

And when they saw, you know, how Mr Lee and his generation really had the steel in them to fight for a better life for all Singaporeans, and how they fought for a fair and just society — they were really moved. And in fact there are many parts of the history that we have not even properly collected. One of the most touching moments for me was, during the tribute event in Tampines, I had a lady who came up to me and said that her father's dying wish, or rather not wish but instruction to her, was that if Mr Lee passed on she would have to attend the wake of Mr Lee every day. For as long as it was held. And she came every day. I saw her.

So when she first told me that I [asked], "What did your father do?" She said "My father was a security officer of Mr Lee. My father saw Mr Lee pushed into the drain by the Communists, and risk his life. My father felt so deeply that that was a generation that really who really risked their life and limbs in order to build Singapore. And in order to build a better life for all Singaporeans. My father reminded us that Mr Lee could have been a successful lawyer working for the British, and would have been rich and comfortable, but he chose otherwise."

So stories like that we haven't even quite collected, much less disseminated. So I fully agree with you. The question is how do we do it in a way that does not come across as "this is just propaganda". And I do think that the way that our schools are beginning to teach it is a lot better. That I think we need to do it in a way that discusses those issues.

I recently met a group of our students who are studying abroad and I shouldn't name where they were studying. And they told me "Oh gee, it's so different. As a secondary school student when we did social studies, we were looking at two things in every source that we were given. The reliability of the source and the accuracy of the source." For reliability the students are taught, "How do you know that this is a reliable source? Is there a bias there, is there a particular angle that this person is trying to put to us?" For the accuracy of a source the question that the students have to answer is, "Are there other sources that you can triangulate, that you can come to check, and does this look reasonable to you? Does all the evidence add up?"

And if you look at our social studies questions, it is of a very different nature. So I don't think we should be so reserved about this, I think we ought to do more.

CHC: Can I add to this minister? Because I have been on this refrain for a long time, that we don't teach history well in school....

BK: I learnt from her.

CHC: We tend to be a little shy about naming our leaders. When Mr S Rajaratnam passed away, many young Singaporeans did not know who he was. When Dr Goh Keng Swee passed away it got a little better but still he was not well known. And I think this is because our histories are written maybe just mentioning them once or twice. They don't become full characters, there is no depth to the person and personalities. And it is a pity because then you don't recall who your founding fathers are, who your leaders are. How do we overcome this? We have to teach history objectively.

BK: Yes.

CHC: Which means you have to talk of Lim Chin Siong, you've got to talk about the PAP coup, you see. And I think you can teach this, and you can teach this well. But I find that perhaps the government's a little defensive on this because, I remember once accompanying DPM Teo Chee Hean, he was then the Minister of Education, to schools in the United States. We went to the magnet schools. And he walked through the classrooms, and there were the US flags all in the front of the classroom.

I said "Minister, I think this is a very good idea, why don't we put a flag in our classrooms in front of the students? The Americans teach patriotism that way." He said "Oh Heng Chee, if we did that people will say it is propaganda."

So I think, unfortunately, this is [the] way that Singapore looks at things. But I feel that's a pity because we should be patriots, we should love our country, we should appreciate our country. But we have to begin by appreciating our history and knowing who our leaders are and inserting their names. So the challenge is to the academics out there in this hall, and there are many of you, and some of you are historians: Please write histories and please write histories that are interesting to read.

HSK: I would agree with all that you have said, Heng Chee, and I would make the same appeal to all of our historians out there. I think that we ought to be objective, but at the same time we ought to inculcate this sense of, this understanding of how Singapore started, why we started, and how did we arrive at where we are today. If we want to understand where do we need to go in the future.

Chairperson: Thank you. Perhaps just a last question from the floor?

Q3: Thank you, [I'm a] community arts activists and advocate. There was one word that has been said by all four speakers throughout this conference, and the word is "trust". All four speakers have said that at one point or another. So in the spirit of trust, with regard to contentious issues, be it LGBT, welfare, or single mothers, equality, inequality — Minister, what is the one real pressure that is facing the government? Rather than skirting around the issue and saying that time is a luxury we can afford to let issues evolve, can we just have a comment from you to say what is the real pressure facing the government from addressing some of the contentious issues? And that is in the interest of trust.

Chairperson: Do you want to specify which contentious issues, otherwise we will be here until tomorrow?

Q3: So specifically it would be the LGBT issue. Just the pressure facing the government, rather than... Mr Ho is a gentleman, he asked the question but he might not say what is the pressure. So you have heard from our side, we want to hear from your side as well — what is the real pressure facing the government? And that's it. Thank you.

HSK: I went speak for the government per se. Let me give my own take on this set of issues.

It is not so much the pressure, but rather it is how we see society coming together to come to agreements on matters [where] people disagree. Societies are very organic, it is not like a machine where you say, "Let me turn the dial and this is the direction, this is how you will go, and let me turn the dial the other way and this is how everyone will accept."

I have seen this even [when] running public sector organisations. You cannot, even in the police force, tell the officers that, you know — even when I was a very young cop many years ago, where command and control was the order of the day — that I have found that when people don't fully subscribe to what you say and what you believe in, the execution will always be very, very poor. And that you end up with all sorts of unintended

121

consequences after you made a decision. And you are talking about an organisation where command and control is the norm.

And over the years as I run public sector organisations, as I discuss with many leaders of organisations about how things really change in your workplace, in your organisation; without fail it is that things change when people truly believe in it. And when people have very different views even within the same organisation, said that, "Well, let us come and debate this, and this is what we agree, we have to do things together, therefore let us agree to do this." And that quality of commitment to a decision makes a huge difference, both to the long-term future of the organisation as well as to the implementation of that decision.

So it is not so much that we are trying to look at this and that, and weigh up this. It is my personal conviction that if people really believe in what they are doing, if they find that there is that meaning in it, they find that this is the right thing to do, they would do it really well. If they don't believe in it and you say, "Well, I will by fiat decide this way or that way", those who disagree will come around to find other ways of either getting back, or find other ways to destroy the decision.

So I hope that we as a society learn how to make decisions that affect everyone. And people will say, "Look, I want my children to be brought up this way" and others will say, "I want my children to be brought up this [other] way." So the issue will not be just for a day or two, it will be an issue that will go across generations. That's why I talk about the quality of relationship. Because if you have that quality of relationship, which is built on a deep understanding of all our points of view, that I told you is a human being face-to-face, and we come to some agreement, we have a far better quality of relationship that will transcend not just a specific issue but will build that kinship that I spoke about.

Chairperson: And on that note it is time for us to wrap up the conference. May I invite the individual speakers just to say something quick and short? Thirty seconds each.

CHC: Amen.

BK: Thank you all, it's time for a drink.

HKP: Ditto.

Chairperson: We've heard a lot from one minister, thank you much.

Home With Heart and Hope[1]

EUGENE K B TAN

As Singapore moves into uncharted waters, how do we protect and grow our precious inheritance of sovereignty, self-determination, and dignity against the backdrop of our society growing in diversity and complexity?

In a more complex environment, how we arrive at a consensus matters tremendously. Political participation must be embraced, and "voice" — understood as more than just the articulation of one's thoughts to include being engaged in the deliberative process of governance — will play a critical role in the process of reaching a consensus or arriving at a decision, without fear or favour.

The government is acutely aware of the growing desire for a more open and vibrant political system — one where the citizen's voice matters, and where the concern and interest with national matters is not the sole preserve of politicians. This politics with a small "p" for the masses is to be distinguished from politics with a big "P" which involves only a select group of citizens partaking in the rough and tumble of adversarial political contests.

Going forward, the need for collaborative governance will only grow in importance — no longer a nice-to-have or simply aspirational, but an abiding imperative. Harnessing the whole society's commitment and drive in the perennial quest for Singapore's relevance to the world will be more purposeful than pulling society along.

---

[1] This essay builds on some of the author's earlier thoughts in "Singapore's Ideational Social Compact: The Compelling, Inclusive Force of Voices in a Plural Society," in Joachim Sim (ed.), *Beyond 50: Re-imagining Singapore* (Singapore: Really Good Books Publishing, 2015), pp. 31–39.

The significant strides made on all fronts have also lulled us into thinking that this very diversity and complexity does not have its own set of issues and challenges. The quest for a forward-looking vision for Singapore — one that epitomises opportunity, hope, fairness, dignity and social solidarity — is not just an exercise of strategic planning. It embodies our belief of how the average Singaporean is very much *a part* of this evolving society, where being *apart* is not a viable option. This is compelling because collaborative governance in nation-building needs to be constantly invigorated, justified and manifested.

As a global city that also needs to be a nation-state, Singapore cannot be just a place (like a hotel). It must be treated as a home even as we continue to require a substantial number of non-citizens in our midst in that common effort to eke a living and endow the hope for a better future.

In this regard, the search for the right balance in terms of the roles of the state, the community and individuals, is crucial. While economic vibrancy remains essential to our wellbeing, the growing desire of Singaporeans for a home with heart and hope patently needs to go beyond rhetoric.

That Singapore must engender within Singaporeans a deep sense of identity, belonging and rootedness to this little red dot we call home, is fundamental to sustaining our sovereignty. This is where the voices of Singaporeans must play a bigger part in our national life. Having Singaporeans willing to spend time, energy and money in advocating causes and values they believe in is important and a meaningful expression of a personal stake vested and intertwined with the larger good. Our nation's future is secure if Singaporeans see their well-being as an integral and intimate part of the nation's.

In the years ahead, we can expect a slew of policy shifts in governance, which may entail a radical rethink of fundamentals that have served us well. The text of our governance must constantly adjust and adapt to the context.

The Our Singapore Conversation (OSC) held between 2012 and 2013 was a massive exercise in consultation, and the response of Singaporeans demonstrated our enthusiasm, maturity and involvement in sharing our views on issues, including "hot-button" ones. We need to have and to be at ease with having more conversations regularly (rather than one Big Conversation), and without their being mediated by the government. This "vertical" conversation has become an accepted aspect of our government communication process, facilitated by REACH, the government feedback unit. But there is tremendous opportunity for a paradigm shift and for significant value creation when Singaporeans develop the habit of speaking with each other and engaging robustly on key issues of the day. These "horizontal" conversations are necessary as issues are increasingly not about what the government thinks is best but rather about what citizens are comfortable with.

In these conversations, *how* we converse with one another matters as much, if not more, as what we converse about. It is about our speaking *with* one another, rather than speaking to or past the other. Even if a meeting of minds cannot be achieved because the differences are too great, the engagement provides a valuable platform to understand the various perspectives on an issue, the vested interests and the possible ways forward. Thus, this process of engagement should not be about sticking to entrenched positions, no matter how principled, but also about how contending groups can co-exist. We should not downplay the "live and let live" mindset; they should operate as a viable segue to more lasting outcomes.

Thus, to keep society thriving and cohesive, we need a recalibration of the roles of the individual, the community and the state. Whether it is about strengthening social safety nets, redefining success beyond academic achievements or the successful helping the less successful, the centrality of collaborative governance, as an exemplar of togetherness, self-reliance and resourcefulness, is a *sine qua non*.

Public policy engagement, deliberation and implementation will be more successful if there is buy-in by the community. This is where co-creation offers the powerful platform for active citizenship to go beyond being a mere concept and rhetoric, to a lived reality that is inherently about collaboration, in which open communication lines between all stakeholders will characterise the partnership.

Co-creation is, in essence, about a government-civil society partnership, with collaboration and cooperation being the hallmarks in the delivery of public services or in the formulation of policies at the municipal and national levels.

Driving this trend is the desire of citizens to be involved and not be a mere digit in policymaking and policy implementation. As a society matures, post-material considerations become more important. People increasingly seek self-fulfilment and self-actualisation, and desire to be consulted on issues that concern them or affect their communities. This sense of involvement and engagement is an important manifestation of active citizenry and a vibrant civil society.

An engaged citizenry, confident that their voices matter, provides the foundation and wherewithal for a more resilient and cohesive society. In short, collaboration is just as much about form as it is substance.

Co-creation in which a range of alternative voices, including critical and opposing voices, is part of the collaborative process, and this implicates purposeful and actionable participation in a community. As we strive to overcome the proverbial mid-life crisis that afflicts nation states more familiar with success than failure, our society stands to gain if it encourages respect for a diversity of voices even at inconvenient times like during a crisis.

As our society matures, the public sphere and public reason acquire greater importance in a deliberative and consultative polity. Besides the formal or institutional process of deliberation that takes place in our legislature, the courts and the executive, there is the equally important process, often informal, of deliberation among citizens. We need to tap this latent source of ideas, passion and beliefs. Dialogue, difference, debate, persuasion and learning in the public sphere are central to political decision-making. A government cannot ignore the weight of citizens' well-informed opinions and reasoned arguments.

A society without a platform for alternative voices loses a vital tool in the moulding of public opinion and developing social solidarity and consensus, the very lifeblood of governance. Our society will be impoverished if there is little or no role for public discourse and reason.

The next 50 years will probably see a withering of the state. This is not simply because the state will be less important. Rather, Singaporeans would desire a fundamental rethink of how Singapore has been governed, a recalibration of state-people relations, as well as getting the balance right on (economic) value vis-à-vis values that define Singapore. This is where we need to arrive at a consensus, and that comes more purposefully from talking with one another, deliberating and recognising that the need to accommodate is not a cop-out. The horizontal conversations are a means to this end.

We can expect some of the major differences or divides in our society to revolve around the different values that motivate and inspire us. Values competition and contestation will feature more prominently in the years ahead. It's the nature of the beast for a society inherently diverse and complex. For a plural society like ours to be sustainable, Singaporeans need to be able to deal with the variety of tempestuous issues with resilience and a willingness to learn from such stresses to the social fabric. Otherwise, a destructive dynamic could be set off in which the unresolved differences, misguided views and prejudices remain to fester and sow discord.

If our past, with the emphasis on economic value, affluence and consumption, had been short on voice options, then the mind-share of our future must embody the growing importance of transcendental pursuits, post-material values and quality of life in which the opportunities to voice and be engaged are critical.

If the focus in the past was overwhelmingly on material well-being, this is unsurprising for a resource-challenged country like Singapore seeking a niche. But material well-being alone at our stage of development cannot build a home, a future, a nation. We should strive, as a nation, to be defined by values rather than by the obsession with value. There is the need to complement the wealth imperative with a sense of belonging, connectedness and meaning in what Singapore stands for and what it means to be a Singaporean.

What must define us are our shared values even if our conversations, vertical and horizontal, become robust and passionate. Shared values discipline and enhance our shared purpose. Our social compact will continue to evolve and be right-sized according to needs, aspirations, and consensus of society. How we manage the competing, and even conflicting, rights, interests and power in the quest for a fair and just society will define the kind of society we will become.

If public discourse and reason are receptive and nurturing of a variety of voices, we can be very confident that this ideational social compact can only enhance what Singapore stands for and what it means to be a true-blue Singaporean.

I believe that more Singaporeans can be encouraged to care enough about our society and so would crave to have a say in how the country is governed. It reflects a better educated, more informed and demanding citizenry who would like to participate in policymaking or, at least, to be heard and to be consulted on matters that affect them. This manifestation of active citizenry is to be encouraged. Increased participation and involvement in Singaporean society provides real and actionable pathways to active citizenship. This hands-on approach is necessary to temper the self-indulgent "navel gazing" and the "me-my-and-mine" value system that is deleterious to nation-building.

Plural Identities, Multiplying Diversity

ELAINE HO

In seeking to address how intercultural understanding can be deepened in Singapore, this panel at Singapore Perspectives (2016) considered the social tensions that might arise from the growing diversity found in our country today. This plurality of identities is an outcome of several factors, including but not limited to new immigration from a wider array of source countries than before; the international mobility of overseas Singaporeans and the global influences they bring; intermarriages between Singaporeans from different ethnic groups and between foreigners and Singaporeans; and the globalisation of the economy, society and popular culture more generally.

While diversity can be approached as a noun (i.e., a condition), the term "diversity" also captures the assembling (i.e., as a verb) of multiple social groups with similar or dissimilar cultural values, and the dynamic ways in which they interact with one another. As Singapore globalises, the diversity represented within it has multiplied compared to the longstanding "Chinese", "Malay", "Indian" and "Others" (CMIO) classification that has guided policies, ranging from politics to housing, education and more both during the post-independence and pre-independence periods (since those classifications originate in colonial policy). Such policies have served us well in many ways, but are the CMIO categorisations underpinning them capacious enough to capture the multiplying faces of diversity in Singapore today?

This was a key question I raised during the conference panel, and my fellow panellists and audience members gamely engaged in lively debate on this topic. One point of view maintains that policies premised on the CMIO classifications safeguard the interests of ethnic minority groups and have successfully cultivated ethnic integration. But can it be that as diversity has multiplied in Singapore, it means we also need to tailor such policies to new realities? For example, living alongside Chinese-Singaporeans are recent Chinese migrants from provinces in Mainland China that are different from the coastal provinces to which Chinese-Singaporeans trace their genealogies. The new Chinese migrants speak another set of regional dialects and enjoy distinctive cuisines associated with their regional affiliation. Likewise, recent Indian migrants have regional affiliations that are more diverse than those familiar to Indian-Singaporeans.

What we are seeing is the multiplication of difference within the "pioneer" ethnic categories associated with earlier waves of settlement and immigration during the pre-independence or immediate post-independence periods. Subsuming the cultural differentiations between co-ethnics under a generalised category of "Chinese" or "Indian" glosses over the multi-dimensional aspects of identity making, such as how ethnicity not only intersects with socio-economic status and religious beliefs — but also nationality status and the significance of pluri-locality (i.e., the multiple affiliations to place in a globalised world). At the same time, the "Others" category under the CMIO framing has been multiplying through the import of temporary migrants, permanent residents and naturalised citizens who come from greater range of countries than before, including within ASEAN such as the Philippines, Indonesia, Vietnam and Myanmar, and internationally from Japan, the United Kingdom, the United States and the European Union.

To be clear, Singapore has always been diverse in its social and cultural composition. The second language policy (also known as the mother tongue language) subsumed plural dialects and regional identities (e.g., Hokkien, Cantonese, or Punjabi and Hindi), while legitimising others that sub-sequently became acknowledged as the official languages of Singapore (i.e., Mandarin, Tamil and Malay along with English). Homogenising identity categorisations are reinforced through language and a range of policies that pervade Singaporean life. Inasmuch as these policies might serve to protect ethnic minority rights or cultivate ethnic integration, they also have the effect of privileging certain racial or cultural attributes that become conflated with natal belonging, which is to associate birthplace with the presumed authenticity of belonging or patriotism.

For example, in one incident dating back to 2014, a locally born athlete felt it necessary to clarify that he is of Eurasian ancestry when he was put in the spotlight, not on account of his athletic achievements, but because members of the public had queried if he is a foreigner on account of his Caucasian features. In this particular incident, the athlete was singled out as someone unsuitable to represent Singapore internationally simply because he *looks different* from the racial groups that are more prominently represented in Singapore (i.e., Chinese, Malay or Indian). This same athlete, Joseph Schooling, was subsequently hailed as a national hero when he won an Olympic gold medal for Singapore in 2016. Yet couched in the acclamations were arguments that continued to legitimise natal belonging and perpetuate hierarchies of authenticity. The key point is, as a sense of "Singaporean identity" has strengthened through the decades, it has created aspects of inclusion for those considered deserving by virtue of their racial attributes, their birthplace, birth right and citizenship (depending on the social situation, these aspects of identity are exercised fluidly). But such premises of inclusion has also made it more prohibitive for deepening attachment amongst those others who do not fit easily into these classifications, which can be detrimental to deepening belonging and patriotism.

Thus far we have restricted our discussion on diversity to those who are resident in Singapore. In the foreseeable future, the globalisation of Singaporeans will also feed into these discussions on the multiplication of difference (including but not limited to ethnicity), natal belonging and patriotism. This can happen in two ways: First, as more Singaporeans go overseas for work, study or lifestyle reasons, they and their children will acquire global identities that become intermeshed with their Singaporean identity. Second-generation Singaporeans who have living abroad since young may be less acquainted with the Singaporean lifestyle and features of its national identity; some may not even be born in Singapore despite holding Singaporean nationality status at birth. Second, as more Singaporeans abroad marry foreigners their children will inherit mixed cultural identities that defy the mainstream ethnic classifications to which we are more accustomed.

Forging ahead we require policies that recognise the multiplying aspects of diversity in Singapore and take seriously the liquidity of social identities. To an extent, policies have evolved by extending the double-barrelled racial classification to children of mixed-race marriages, and on a case-by-case basis allowing second language learning that is not restricted to the officially recognised racial identity of a student. Yet, more can be done if only we come round to appreciating more fully the multiplying faces of diversity in Singapore at the workplace, housing, schools and other spheres of life. This need not mean compromising equality and the recognition of existing minority rights, particularly political rights. Rather it means holding those minority rights in view while simultaneously crafting policies and nurturing a Singaporean identity that is adept at managing not only economic change but also social fluidity as the country's social composition evolves. Recognising the multiplying aspects of diversity in Singapore and its implications for policymaking brings us closer towards cultivating respect for a wider range of minority groups as aligned with the changing social fabric of Singaporean society, and instilling in them a stronger sense of stakeholdership in Singapore.

Moving beyond Tolerance

HASSAN AHMAD

As in everything, diversity brings blessings and burden. If managed well, it would bring benefits. If taken lightly, it could breed bedlam.

It was obvious that very little, if any, was raised by the participating audience, on the more prevalent and pressing issues such as increased religiosity and migration that pose as risks to social cohesiveness. Perhaps Singaporeans are of the impression that these are not issues facing a friendly and diplomatically-savvy country; or it is a reflection of their high confidence in the government to deal with the matter effectively, if need be.

"UNUSUAL, UNNATURAL STATE OF AFFAIRS"

Singapore is one of the smallest countries in the world, yet it is a sanctuary to the largest number of faiths. The Global Religious Diversity (GRD) Report, ranked us as the most diverse, in terms of religions, out of 232 countries. Prime Minister Lee Hsien Loong had earlier shared that "this is an unusual, unnatural state of affairs."

This young island-state has gotten most part of its politics and policies right thus far. Since the riots in the 1960s, the nation had learnt and went on to enjoy remarkable harmony, where inter-racial and inter-religious co-existence are concerned. The Housing & Development Board (HDB) policy and the GRC system, *inter alia*, ensured ethnic representations in both living and ruling environments. These help built the foundation for integration.

In the active pursuit and exploration of new formulae for national excellence and global success, Singapore has made bold ventures, *inter alia*, the SAP school system, which have been repeatedly questioned, including by student beneficiaries of that system. Exclusivity isolates those involved from the wider society, as they mix within a narrow social circle. To some extent, it disables them from greater exposure and arrests their social skills and circles. In parallel, the status and long-term consequences of full-time Madrasahs here should be reviewed and vetted on the same page as the SAP schools.

TERRORISM

There are no guarantees to sustained peace and harmony in any society. In this respect, Singapore is better off than most nations. But no nation is immune to terrorism. While everyone has a duty and role in the fight against terrorism, the core the strategy must be community engagement and education — progressively building a strong and sincere network of trust amongst the different denominations.

The many arrests last year, though unrelated, of two Singaporean youths and 27 Bangladeshi nationals working in Singapore, are evidence that terror elements are no longer facing Singapore at her front door, but already in her backyard. Fortunately, sound legislations, systems and mechanisms are well in place to detect, act or react against threats of terror.

EFFECTS OF EXTREMISM ON INTER-FAITH RELATIONS

Matters of religion have always been dicey and have had deep faultlines, and they have become more complex. With the ever-growing reach of and penetration by the social media, people are more exposed, hence more vulnerable to extreme ideologies, where the sources stemmed from differing landscapes, histories, cultures and challenges, hence the doctrinal interpretations.

Extremism may not advocate violence, but it is as sharp and pointed to cut through the social fabric and jeopardise harmony and integration. For example, some Muslim scholars prohibited the extending of festive greetings to non-Muslims on their festive occasions. Separately, there is an increasing fixation on and promotion of "halal" consciousness in recent times, that have extended way beyond the fundamental teachings of the faith. Such extremisms have caused awkwardness in the dealings between Muslims and subscribers of other faiths.

MIGRATION ON INTRA-FAITH

The influx of migrants is an inevitable necessity for Singapore's continued growth, but with it comes the risk of adding load to the cultural, and more so, the religious faultlines. For example, Catholics from the Philippines may continue to keep their spiritual compass aligned to the Archbishop there, or the Muslims from South Asia or West Asia may continue to hold firmly to their school of thoughts where doctrinal interpretations, based on their cultures or heritage, may be inappropriate for practice in this part of the world.

DON'T TOLERATE, ACCEPT

There is a real need to emphasise on the most fundamental of similarities, based on good morals including compassion and peace. Social cohesion requires civic engineering. There needs to be platforms for Singaporeans — native, new or naturalised — to have real exchanges to better acquaint, educate, understand, appreciate and accept each other's differences, especially given that the most number of faiths of the world is squeezed into one of the littlest nation.

Interestingly, Social Studies, along with subjects in the Humanities, is now a compulsory and examinable subject in secondary schools. Back in the 1980s, secondary schools introduced Religious Knowledge as an examinable subject at GCE "O" Levels. Perhaps the Education Ministry might be sufficiently bold to inject Inter-Faith Knowledge into the current Social Studies syllabus. Concurrently, the Defence and Home ministries could introduce a subject on Inter-Faith Appreciation as part of its Basic Training and/or Officer Cadets courses for active NSMen and reservists. National Service is where some parents' sons, some siblings' brothers, some school-mates' buddies, some girls' boyfriends and some families' relatives, could benefit from a common and mandatory platform. Such knowledge and exposure would serve the individuals, their families and the nation well, when the NSmen step into the working world, marriage life, parenthood and other leadership roles.

Last, people must refrain from using the term or having to "tolerate" other religious practices, as it connotes negativity in relationships. As Singaporeans walk and work towards sustained racial and religious harmony, they must learn and live to accept and appreciate their differences. Otherwise, cohesive diversity would only be limited to an attractive term or concept.

Inclusive Growth, Social Protection and the Big Gaps and Risks in Singapore's Social Policy

YEOH LAM KEONG

In my session on "Inclusive Growth" with Minister Ong Ye Kung, I brought up several key points on concrete social policy reform that would greatly increase social well-being and lead to truly inclusive growth in Singapore. These could greatly aid Singapore evolving towards the kind of caring and cohesive society we would want our children and grandchildren to grow up in, substantially increasing the sense of "happiness, prosperity and progress" enunciated in our National pledge, and could be the basis of social cohesion and national identity — the elusive but all-important sense of "we" that was the theme of Institute of Policy Studies (IPS) Singapore Perspectives 2016.

These reforms are in six key policy areas: Social security, education, public housing, healthcare, public transport and population policy. I set out fiscally affordable, measurable KPIs that government could work towards in these areas and asked him why we were not heading more decisively towards these policy targets, which were clearly public goods and needed strong government initiative and financing.

Just to recap, these six key social policy directions and KPIs are:

1. Reform social security to eradicate absolute poverty and ensure retirement adequacy, especially for low-income citizens. I further specified that we could make a huge start here by raising the Workfare Income Supplement (WIS) and Silver Support Scheme (SSS) to S$500–S$600 a month from current inadequate levels at a cost of less than 2% of GDP in the long term (we have an under-

lying structural budget surplus of 6–7% of GDP). This would largely eliminate much of absolute poverty among the working and elderly poor.

2. Ensure affordable public housing that takes 10–15 years to repay and also include sufficient availability of cheap rental flats for those whose circumstances did not allow ownership — especially for the poor.

3. Make social mobility an important objective in our education system and create a "creativity-heavy, tuition-light system" that meets the needs of the new knowledge economy.

4. Achieve a public transport system at least as good as Hong Kong's.

5. Announce and implement a proper universal long-term care and chronic primary care system vital for our rapidly ageing population — present in most OECD countries but missing in Singapore.

6. Commit to a final population "well below 6.9 million" as enunciated by the Prime Minister in the Parliamentary Debate on the Population White Paper.

Minister Ong handled my comments and questions very smoothly. He assured the audience and me that he was largely "on my side" in the debate and agreed with these directions for social policy and in most cases couldn't disagree with the above policy objectives. I believe he was sincere when he said this.

In reality however, such needed reforms are likely to proceed at a crawl, albeit in the right direction. The Minister himself, while impeccably intentioned and informed, has probably little say in changing this situation. He clearly enunciated the many initiatives on the ground trying to achieve the same objectives and showed keen awareness of the many policy debates around many of them. But at the end of the day he too, has to work within the policy constraints that slow these reforms down.

While well-intentioned, policy reform seems to be hampered to a crawl by several structural forces.

First, there is an ideological policy distrust of any form of income based welfare at the most senior levels of government, based more on belief and mindset than empirical evidence that most forms of welfare are bad and will seriously undermine independence and incentive to work.

Second is the belief that welfare benefits, once given, are a slippery slope to the irresistible demands by the middle class for more handouts that will end in fiscal unsustainability.

Third is a natural policy inertia by a bureaucracy that is slow to make transformative change to make social policy future-ready. Unfortunately, the foundations of current social policy were laid in a very different operating environment. Real wages were robustly rising, families had several children and thus potential income earners, recession was much more infrequent (two in the first 30 years of independence compared to four over the last 15 years), inequality was lower both here and globally and the global financial, and trade and technological orders were much more stable.

None of these conditions are likely to pertain in future — much more likely the opposite. Wages have tended to stagnate in advanced countries as competition from the vast workforces of the emerging world, and info-comm and Artificial Intelligence-enabled labour-replacing technology create vast technological unemployment. Income and wealth inequality has risen to historically extreme levels with no signs of abating. Demography will shrink family sizes below replacement rates, placing huge burdens on the working young to support their retiring baby boomer parents, many of whom have inadequate savings and education to support their own retirement.

Adequate social protection is urgently needed in all developed countries to shield their populations from these forces in the inevitable engagement with global capitalism. And nowhere more so than in Singapore, one of the most open and globalised economies in the world.

Meantime, with reform in crawl mode there is a high and rising social and political cost. We have seen in the UK with Brexit, and in the US with the possible election of Donald Trump,[1] that a disenfranchised, insecure electorate that loses trust in politics and policy credibility and hope for positive change in this new globalised environment can vote irrationally, in favour of destructive policy and political instability. Indeed, the international economic, trade, financial and security order are now increasingly at risk from this destructive politics of hopelessness.

---

[1] This was written before Donald Trump was elected as the 45th President of the United States of America.

So far it has been the countries with adequate social protection — not just the Nordics, bit also a range of social democracies in much of Northern Europe, Canada, Australia and New Zealand that have escaped the worst of this destructive populism.

Singapore needs to take urgent heed. Policy trust and political credibility is much more vital for us than in the US or the UK, where a huge domestic and regional economy is a natural buffer for resilience. Doing big, difficult things together as one people is an ability that more than any other has ensured both our survival and our success. We cannot afford to lose it.

So can we afford to keep the social policy reforms like I have outlined in "crawl" mode? I believe not and that we are taking a far bigger risk with our polity and social fabric than we realise if we continue to do so.

The irony is that of all OECD countries, we are currently the best endowed to craft a holistic, fiscally sustainable and economically dynamic and intelligent social protection system based on the six key reforms I outlined.

First, as pointed out in the forum the Singapore government already owns 80% of our land area. Second, it has more fiscal headroom than any other developed country. It starts with a huge structural surplus and massive foreign reserves per capita. It has one of the best civil services in the world and many positive examples to learn from.

More than any other developed nation, we can transform social policy to give us the security, happiness and social progress that comes with true prosperity, even in the face of the unforgiving forces of globalisation.

Yes we can. And we can afford it. So why don't we?

Inclusive Growth and Restructuring

CHUA HAK BIN

Over the last eight years or so, the government has significantly shifted its policy towards the broader objective of more "inclusive growth" from just "top-line GDP growth." Some would place the watershed year as the 2008 elections, during which People's Action Party (PAP) saw their popular vote plummet to 60%, the lowest since independence. Some would draw the timeline as being slightly earlier, possibly 2007 when the government introduced Workfare, a quasi-welfare scheme that supplements the wages of lower-wage workers. This was quite a departure from the anti-welfare and anti-dependency philosophy, particularly during Lee Kuan Yew's time.

Economic restructuring and shift towards a more inclusive and more productivity-driven growth is ongoing, with the results so far somewhat mixed. The expansion of the social safety net has clearly raised the income and well-being of lower-income households. Such measures included Workfare, MediShield Life, GST rebates, Pioneer Generation Package, more generous Housing & Development Board (HDB) grants and a more progress income tax system. To be clear, there was already a social support scheme in place before the shift to "left of centre", but the support was historically heavily concentrated in the form of generous HDB housing grants and subsidies. A HDB ownership-centred social support system however allocates a larger proportion of government funding for the lower-middle and middle classes. Lower-income households, especially the lowest 10%, were least able to capitalise on the generous HDB subsidies, either because of their low and unstable wages or being unable to afford even the small down-payment. Proportions of the housing subsidies were moreover higher with HDB prices, benefiting the middle class more.

There is little disagreement on most of these social support measures to improve the "inclusivity" from growth. Wages of lower-income households were under pressure from globalisation and the opening up of China and India. Income inequality was worsening, as growth was disproportionately benefiting higher-income more than lower-income households. In some of the pre-Global Financial Crisis (GFC) years, real wages in the lowest household segment were even falling despite GDP growth being above 6% (Chua, 2007). The government's fiscal position was robust and improving, especially when growth was strong, and could readily afford a larger allocation towards social support schemes. Recent metrics of income inequality and wages of lower-income households have improved with these social transfers, especially from the sharp increase in healthcare subsidies.

The more controversial restructuring policies are probably the stricter foreign worker and immigration policies, as well as the productivity initiatives. A myriad of policies became tangled up and defended as being supportive of "inclusive growth". Immigration and foreign workers were often blamed for causing unequal growth and crowding-out citizens. Nationalist sentiments intensified the "Singaporeans first" sentiment, where policies became more discriminating and differentiated on the treatment of Singaporeans, permanent residents and foreigners. Some of the debates took on an ideological bent.

First, redistributive policies need not come completely at the expense of growth. Standard macro-textbook models teach us that the objectives of "growth" versus "equality" can be maximised and pursued separately. The optimal strategy is to maximise growth and welfare, and then re-distribute those gains via "lump sum transfers" to achieve a fairer income distribution without distorting prices or wages. Measures such as the workfare scheme, GST or utility rebates and Central Provident Fund (CPF) top-ups can be counted as part of the "lump sum transfers" in this category of support measures. In reality however, there are many other government policies, including taxes, quotas and regulations that distort market prices, returns and incentives to investment and employment.

Second, the argument that foreign labour is a *substitute* (rather than *complement*) for resident labour has not been validated in the post-restructuring years. There are clearly many jobs that Singaporeans do not want to work in, but where such sectors are important for the economy. A tight labour market and low resident unemployment rate also imply that one sector's gain is another's loss. Stricter foreign worker policies via levies and quotas (dependency ratio ceilings) has instead raised business costs and deterred private investments.

One of the disturbing statistics over the past two years is the contraction in private investments. This is occurring despite generous government grants and subsidies for investments in productivity initiatives. Private fixed capital formation contracted 1.6% in 2015 and 5% in 2014. The contraction was not just driven by property investments, but also by machinery & equipment and intellectual property products. The latter is all the more alarming given the push for greater R&D and innovation to drive productivity. Economic Development Board's (EDB) measure of fixed asset commitments (FAI) likewise contracted by 2.5% in both 2014 and 2015. And for 2016, EDB is forecasting FAI to plunge by 13% to 30%.

Growth and productivity are more negatively impacted with the restructuring, when foreign labour is more a *complement* to resident labour. Demand for local workers is negatively impacted when businesses shut or downsize. Companies are struggling to find the available resident labour to meet the quota requirements. Another disturbing statistic is the recent sharp increase in business closures, already *exceeding* the numbers seen during the 2008 GFC. Business closures rose by over 7% in 2015 over 2014; and by about 113% from January to April 2016 from the same period a year ago.

Third, the productivity drive, so far, has been a failure. Growth in labour productivity has been *negative* for the last four years, averaging −0.1% for the period 2011–2015. This is well short of the 2%–3% target set at the start of the productivity drive. The dismal outcome is despite the generous S$3 billion plus Productivity and Innovation Credit Scheme, which has not revived private investments or boosted labour productivity growth. Why labour productivity has been so weak remains a big question mark. Schemes that incentivised the replacement of more productive foreign labour with less productive resident labour may be hurting overall productivity (although some would argue that this is a better *social* outcome). There is probably some merit in questioning whether the complex regime of foreign worker levies and quotas have distorted the labour market to such an extent that productivity improvements are hampered. It remains to be seen whether the S$1 billion (a year) SkillsFuture scheme or the S$19 billion (over five years) R&D plan under the National Research Foundation, will have any visible impact on aggregate labour productivity and growth in the coming years.

The productivity-driven growth model was initially targeted to hit about 3%–5% growth, of which productivity growth was to contribute 2%–3% and labour force growth 1%–2%. The growth target has steadily fallen over the years. Achieving even a productivity growth target of 1%–2%, while more realistic, remains somewhat elusive after four years of negative growth. GDP growth forecasts have settled at around 2%, a steep fall from the 7% seen during the high-growth episode pre-GFC. Lower growth will impact fiscal revenue and capacity at which the government can increase social transfers in the future — all the more challenging in the face of an ageing population and slowing workforce growth.

Manufacturing is a major casualty from the restructuring and tight foreign worker policy. Manufacturing has slid from a peak of about 20.5% of GDP in 2011 to 17.8% in 2015, the lowest since 1997 during the Asian financial crisis. There are growing concerns that loss of the manufacturing base will also impact future productivity and reduce the diversity of Singapore's economy. Scope for productivity gains are far larger in manufacturing than services. There are potential demand and knowledge externalities that may be lost as the manufacturing sector shrinks both in terms of jobs and production. There is a huge risk that the resources committed and government effort deployed over the past decades to create and sustain a manufacturing core may be rapidly eroded and wasted by the end of this decade.

Balancing growth and equity is a difficult tradeoff. Singapore has probably surrendered 2%–3% annual growth over the past seven to eight years from the economic "restructuring", in exchange for the pursuit of more "inclusive growth". Ballpark estimates suggest that the opportunity cost in GDP terms is in the magnitude of about S$50 billion to S$70 billion in aggregate over the past seven years. The government could have captured about a fifth of these gains, S$10–S$14 billion, money that could have gone some ways to further improve the social safety net.

Restructuring and tight foreign worker policies have taken a heavier toll on growth, private investment and the manufacturing sector than previously thought. Productivity initiatives have not improved labour productivity.

Blaming foreign labour for poor labour productivity in the previous decade has not been supported by the post-restructuring experience. Complex foreign labour measures may instead be distorting labour markets and hurting productivity. Rather, the fall in private investment despite generous productivity grants, suggests that foreign labour is more a complement than substitute, to domestic labour.

Increasing social transfers and healthcare subsidies has reduced income inequality and improved the social safety net. Social spending has risen to about 8% of GDP in 2015 from 6% just four years ago, while public healthcare spending's share of GDP has more than doubled over the same period (to about 2.3% of GDP). But the extent to which government transfers can continue in the future will be impacted by slowing growth and an ageing population, short of a productivity miracle. Expenditure needs are growing faster than fiscal revenue over the last few years and the longer-term picture will be even more challenging. A rebalancing of the growth equation and tradeoffs may be necessary to sustain a higher growth path, which allows for growing social transfers in the face of an ageing population and slower growing resident workforce.

REFERENCE

Chua, HB (2007). Singapore economy: The new and the dual. In Tan, TH (Ed.), *Singapore Perspectives 2007*, pp. 7–23. Singapore: World Scientific.

About the Contributors

CHAN Chun Sing is currently the Secretary-General of the National Trades Union Congress (NTUC) and Minister in the Prime Minister Office. On 1 October 2015, Mr Chan was appointed Deputy Chairman of the People's Association. He relinquished his previous duties in the Ministry of Social and Family Development (MSF) and Ministry of Defence on 9 April 2015 to join NTUC full-time. At MSF, he was responsible for improving social service delivery, enhancing social safety nets and strengthening support for families in Singapore. On 8 April 2015, the NTUC Central Committee unanimously elected him to be NTUC Secretary-General from 4 May 2015 to help strengthen labour leadership at NTUC and the link between the labour movement and the government. He was re-elected as the NTUC Secretary-General by the NTUC National Delegates' Conference on 29 October 2015.

David CHAN is Lee Kuan Yew Fellow, Professor of Psychology and Director of the Behavioural Sciences Institute at the Singapore Management University (SMU), Adjunct Principal Scientist at the Agency for Science, Technology and Research (A*STAR), and Co-Director of the Centre for Technology and Social-Behavioural Insights, a research centre jointly established by A*STAR and SMU. He has received numerous international awards and is the first non-American to receive the Distinguished Early Career Contributions Award from the Society for Industrial and Organisational Psychology (SIOP). He was ranked ninth worldwide in the list of Top 100 most published researchers of the 1990s in the top journals of I-O Psychology. His works have been cited over 3,000 times in journal articles in various disciplines. He has authored or edited six books. He has served as editor or board member on several journals. He is Consultant to numerous organisations in the public, private and people sectors in Singapore and the United States. He is a member of the National Council on Problem Gambling (NCPG), Governing Board for the Workplace Safety and Health Institute, International Panel of Experts as well as Research and Development Advisory Panel for the Urban Redevelopment Authority, International Advisory Panel for the Singapore Workforce Development Agency; a Director on the boards for the Agri-Food and Veterinary Authority of Singapore and Singapore Corporation of Rehabilitative Enterprises; and Chairman of the International Advisory Panel to the NCPG and National Addictions Management Service. He is recipient of the Outstanding Volunteer Award presented by the Ministry of Social and Family Development. He is an invited columnist for *The Straits Times* and consultant to *Channel NewsAsia* on the five-part programme series *Social Experiments* and the five-part programme series *Days of Disasters*. He is an Elected Fellow of SIOP, the American Psychological Association, the Association for Psychological Science and the International Association of Applied Psychology.

CHAN Heng Chee is currently Ambassador-at-Large with the Singapore Ministry of Foreign Affairs and Chairman of the Lee Kuan Yew Centre for Innovative Cities in the Singapore University of Technology and Design (SUTD). She is Chairman of the National Arts Council and a Member of the Presidential Council for Minority Rights. Ambassador Chan served as Singapore's Ambassador to the United States from 1996 to 2012 and Singapore's Permanent Representative to the United Nations from 1989 to 1991. She was concurrently High Commissioner to Canada and Ambassador to Mexico. Previously, she was Executive Director of the Singapore International Foundation (which created a Singapore version of the Peace Corps) and Director of the Institute of Southeast Asian Studies. She was the Founding Director of the Institute of Policy Studies and Head of the Department of Political Science, National University of Singapore. Ambassador Chan was awarded a Doctor of Laws by the University of Warwick (United Kingdom), a Doctor of Letters by the University of Newcastle (Australia), and a Doctor of Letters by the University of Buckingham (United Kingdom). She was named Singapore's first Woman of the Year in 1991, and was twice awarded the National Book Awards in 1986 for *A Sensation of Independence: A Political Biography of David Marshall*, and in

1978 for *The Dynamics of One Party Dominance: The PAP at the Grassroots*. When Ambassador Chan left Washington DC at the end of her appointment, she received the Inaugural Asia Society Outstanding Diplomatic Achievement Award, the Inaugural Foreign Policy Outstanding Diplomatic Achievement Award 2012 and the United States Navy Distinguished Public Service Award. Ambassador Chan holds a BSocSc (First Class Hons) from the National University of Singapore, a MA from Cornell University and a PhD from the University of Singapore.

CHUA Hak Bin is currently a consultant with the Economics & Investment Strategy department at GIC. He was formerly the Head of Emerging Asia and ASEAN Economics at Bank of America Merrill Lynch for about six years. He has also worked as a Strategist and Economist at Citi, Deutsche Private Wealth Management, DBS Bank and RHB Bank. Prior to joining the private sector, Dr Chua was with the Monetary Authority of Singapore for about six years, heading the external economies, financial surveillance and planning, policy & communications divisions. In Kuala Lumpur, he was overseeing corporate finance for a listed property, construction and plantation company. He holds a PhD in Economics from Harvard University, a Bachelor of Science in Electrical Engineering, and a Bachelor of Arts in Economics from Brown University. Dr Chua was a Visiting Lecturer in International Economics at Yale University for a year after completing his PhD.

Janadas DEVAN, Director of the Institute of Policy Studies, was educated at the National University of Singapore and Cornell University in the United States. He was a journalist, writing for *The Straits Times* and broadcasting for Radio Singapore International, before being appointed the government's Chief of Communications at the Ministry of Communications and Information in 2012. He is now concurrently Deputy Secretary at the Prime Minister's Office.

Walter FERNANDEZ is the Editor-in-Chief of MediaCorp Pte Ltd. A Singapore Press Holdings scholar, he started his career in journalism in 1995 at *The Straits Times*, writing on both politics and economics. He rose to be one of the paper's senior correspondents and was seconded to help then Minister Mentor Lee Kuan Yew with his memoirs. He joined MediaCorp in 2001 as the Night Editor at *Channel NewsAsia* Singapore where he was responsible for its flagship local news bulletin *Singapore Tonight*. In 2004, he took over as Executive Editor of *Channel NewsAsia* International, overseeing the channel's correspondents and international coverage. In 2006, Mr Fernandez joined *TODAY* as its Editor and in July 2013 he was appointed Editor-in-Chief, overseeing all news and current affairs content across all of MediaCorp's television, newspaper, radio and digital platforms.

Warren FERNANDEZ is Editor of *The Straits Times*, Singapore's best-selling English daily newspaper. He joined the paper in 1990 as a Political Reporter and rose to become News Editor. He later also served as Foreign Editor and Deputy Editor. He left to join Royal Dutch Shell in 2008 as a Global Manager for its Future Energy project, before returning to the paper in February 2012 as its Editor. He graduated with First Class Honours from Oxford University, where he read Philosophy, Politics and Economics, and also has a Masters in Public Administration from Harvard University's John F. Kennedy School of Government. Both degrees were obtained on Singapore Press Holdings scholarships. He has written several books, including *Lee Kuan Yew: The Man and His Ideas*; *Thinking Allowed: Fear, Politics and Change in Singapore*; *Without Fear or Favour: 50 Years of the Public Service Commission*; *Our Homes: 50 Years of Housing a Nation*; *Men for Others*; and most recently, *Lead Your Life!* He was also part of the editorial team that assisted Mr Lee Kuan Yew with his two-part memoir, *The Singapore Story*. He had served on various national committees, including the Cost Review Committee, the Remaking Singapore Committee, Singapore 21, and Compass, as well as on boards of directors for the National Environment Agency, the Civil Service College, and the Energy Studies Institute. Currently, he is a Board Member of the National Parks Board, National Heritage Board, Straits Times (Overseas) Ltd, Straits Times Press Pte Ltd as well as the Chairman of The Straits Times School Pocket Money Fund.

HASSAN Ahmad, is the Technical Adviser and Executive Director of the Corporate Citizen Foundation, a private sector alliance for regional humanitarian disaster relief and development. Concurrently, he holds the corporate portfolio of Director, Philanthropy & Sustainability of HSL Constructor, a Singaporean foreshore and marine engineering group. As the Head of Mercy Relief and Lien Aid (2003–2013), Mr Hassan has extensive field experience in disaster management and sustainable community development for disadvantaged and disaster-prone communities across 24 countries in Asia. His work warrants the engagement of the various segments of societies at the countries he serves. In 2008, he completed a United Nations policy review with the Stockholm International Peace Research Institute on the Effectiveness of Foreign Military Assets in Natural Disasters. Locally, he serves as the District Councillor for the Southeast Community Development Centre and as a volunteer to the Inter-Religious Organisation Singapore. A law-trained road warrior, Mr Hassan firmly believes that the world's future hinges on the proper management of the development and progress of rural communities. He enlivens his humanitarian commitment by serving with passion on the adamantine that "he who serves others, serves himself last". His youth development included serving in the hospitality, design and concept, marketing and law enforcement services in the private and public sectors.

HENG Swee Keat is the Minister for Finance and Member of Parliament for Tampines GRC. The Ministry of Finance manages the national budget, oversees corporate governance regulations, and supervises the prudent investment and utilisation of public funds and government reserves. Mr Heng is the Chairman of a national committee that is studying strategies for Singapore's future economy. He is also the Deputy Chairman of the National Research Foundation, which sets the direction for Singapore's research, innovation and enterprise strategies. Before this, Mr Heng served as Minister for Education from 2011 to 2015. He drove programmes for a student-centric, values-driven education system, emphasising the holistic development of students and multiple educational pathways. While at MOE, Mr Heng also led *Our Singapore Conversation*, a national consultation exercise that reached out to close to 50,000 Singaporeans on their aspirations for Singapore's future. In 2015, he chaired the Singapore 50 (SG50) Steering Committee leading the celebrations for Singapore's Golden Jubilee. Prior to entering politics in May 2011, Mr Heng was the Managing Director of the Monetary Authority of Singapore, where he received the

"Central Bank Governor of the Year in Asia-Pacific" Award by the British magazine *The Banker*. He has served in various other public service positions, including appointments in the Singapore Police Force, as the Permanent Secretary of the Ministry of Trade and Industry, as the Chief Executive Officer of the Trade Development Board, and as the Principal Private Secretary to the then-Senior Minister Lee Kuan Yew from 1997 to 2000. In 2001, Mr Heng was awarded the Gold Medal in Public Administration, and the Meritorious Medal in 2010 for his contribution to the public service in Singapore. Mr Heng graduated with an MA in Economics from Cambridge University in the United Kingdom. He also holds a Master of Public Administration from the Kennedy School of Government, Harvard University.

Elaine HO is Associate Professor at the Department of Geography, National University of Singapore (NUS). Her research addresses how citizenship is changing as a result of transnational migration. She has conducted research in China, Myanmar and Singapore. Her current research projects focus on African student migration to China and border mobility between Myanmar and China. Prior to joining NUS, she was a Lecturer at the University of Leeds. She completed her PhD at University College London, after which she was awarded postdoctoral fellowships at Royal Holloway University of London and the University of British Columbia. Associate Professor Ho serves on the editorial boards of *Citizenship Studies*, *Emotions, Society and Space*, and the *Singapore Journal of Tropical Geography*. She is also an international member of the Peer Review College established by the Economic and Social Research Council, United Kingdom.

HO Kwon Ping is Executive Chairman of Singapore-listed Banyan Tree Holdings; Chairman of Bangkok-listed Thai Wah Public Company Ltd; and the founding Chairman of Singapore Management University (SMU). Born in 1952, Mr Ho received his university education in Tung Hai University, Taiwan; Stanford University, California and the University of Singapore. He has also been awarded honorary doctorates from Johnson and Wales University (2000) and The Hong Kong Polytechnic University (2015). He worked as a broadcast and financial journalist and was the Economics Editor of the *Far Eastern Economic Review* in Hong Kong. He joined the family business, Thai Wah and Wah-Chang, in 1981. In 1994, after the successful rehabilitation of an abandoned tin mine into Laguna Phuket, Asia's first integrated resort, he launched Banyan Tree Hotels and Resorts. Banyan Tree owns and manages more than 40 hotels and resorts, 70 spas and 80 retail galleries and three golf courses in over 20 countries. Two other integrated resorts: Laguna Bintan (Indonesia) and Laguna LangCo (Vietnam), are part of the group. Mr Ho received the London Business School Entrepreneurship Award in 2005. In 2008, he was named CEO of the Year at the Singapore Corporate Awards, and in 2009, he was the recipient of the Hospitality Lifetime Achievement Award at the China Hotel Investment Summit in Shanghai. In 2010, he became the first Asian to receive the ACA (American Creativity Association) Lifetime Achievement Award in recognition of his creativity and innovation in various spheres of endeavour. In 2012, Mr Ho received the CNBC Travel Business Leader Award Asia Pacific. As Chairman of SMU, Mr Ho was awarded the Singapore Government's Meritorious Service Medal for his contribution in the founding of SMU. In 2015, he published his first book *The Ocean in a Drop*, compiled from his lectures as the inaugural IPS-Nathan Fellow for the Study of Singapore, named after Singapore's sixth President. Mr Ho is married to Ms Claire Chiang, Senior Vice President, Banyan Tree Holdings. They have three children — two sons and a daughter, and welcomed their first grandchild in 2015.

Bilahari KAUSIKAN retired in June 2013 and is currently Ambassador-at-Large and Policy Adviser in the Ministry of Foreign Affairs. From 2001 to May 2013, Ambassador Kausikan was first the Second Permanent Secretary and then Permanent Secretary of the Ministry of Foreign Affairs. Ambassador Kausikan has also served as the Permanent Representative to the United Nations in New York and as Ambassador to the Russian Federation. Raffles Institution, the University of Singapore and Columbia University in New York all attempted to educate Ambassador Kausikan.

Vikram KHANNA is Associate Editor of *The Business Times*, where he has worked since 1993. Prior to that he was an Economist at the International Monetary Fund in Washington DC, where he spent seven years. A Singaporean, Mr Khanna has spent more than 28 years of his life in

Singapore. During that time, he has served on several government commit-tees, including the Economic Review Committee of 2001, the Pro-Enterprise Panel and The Enterprise Challenge. He is a prolific writer and has conducted more than 200 full-length interviews with global chief executive officers, government leaders and thought leaders from around the world. Mr Khanna serves on the Board of The Substation, an independent arts centre, and is on the Council of the Economic Society of Singapore. He has BA, MA and MPhil degrees in Economics from the University of Cambridge, United Kingdom.

KOK Heng Leun is a bilingual theatre director in Singapore and the Artistic Director of Drama Box. He has directed over 80 productions, and his directorial works have been shown in India, Macau, Taiwan, Austria and Shanghai. Mr Kok is an advocate for applied and engaged arts, and is recognised as one of Asia's foremost Forum Theatre practitioners. In recent years, he has actively promoted cultural exchanges and dialogues among artists and cultural workers in the region as well as internationally. He teaches in schools, higher institutions and conducts master classes in directing, including in Macau and recently at the prestigious La MaMa International Director Seminar in Italy. He has also played an important role in transferring Theatre of the Oppressed skills to Taiwan by fostering a sustained interest in the art form in Taipei. A strong believer of research and documentation of theatre and performance, he has initiated various projects to document and research on Chinese language theatre in Singapore. These include *SCENES: Singapore's Chinese Language Theatre*, a curated festival programme of theatre and exhibitions, a published anthology of contempo-rary Singapore Chinese language plays, and the co-conceptualisation of a publication on the history of Singapore's Chinese language theatre. He is currently Artistic Consultant to Gu-Ling-Street Avant Theatre in Taipei; Artistic Consultant for the Macau Arts Festival; and Advisor to Jana Sanskriti International Research and Resource Institute in India.

LEE Huay Leng is Editor of *Lianhe Wanbao* and Senior Vice President (New Growth) of *Lianhe Zaobao*. She also teaches at the National University of Singapore as an Adjunct Assistant Professor at the Department of Chinese Studies. She started her journalistic career in *Lianhe Zaobao* in

1994 upon graduation. She was with the paper for 20 years in different roles as Sports Reporter, Political Reporter, Hong Kong Correspondent, Beijing Bureau Chief, China Editor, News Editor and Deputy Editor. For public service, Ms Lee serves as a Member of Public Transport Council, Board Member of the National Environment Agency, Board Director of the National Kidney Foundation and Member of the Founders' Memorial Committee.

Justin LEE is a Research Fellow at the Institute of Policy Studies. He has substantive interests in issues related to disadvantaged and vulnerable populations, and has done research on the social inclusion of people with disabilities, proper end-of-life planning for vulnerable seniors and the re-integration of ex-offenders. He is also interested in the non-profit sector at large, specifically on developments that affect the state of philanthropy, social services and various other community assets in Singapore. He pays keen attention to the role and strengths of new and untapped resources — such as game designers, community artists and other social innovators — that can be harnessed to address complex social problems. He is also Chair-person of ArtsWok Collaborative, a non-profit organisation engaged in arts-based community development projects that seek to build the capacity of socially-engaged arts groups through training, research and advocacy. He has a PhD in Sociology from the University of California, Los Angeles.

NG Chee Meng is currently Minister for Education (Schools) and Second Minister for Transport. He was appointed to the Cabinet of Singapore as Acting Minister for Education (Schools) and Senior Minister of State for Transport on 1 October 2015. Prior to his Cabinet appointment, he served as Singapore's Chief of Defence Force (CDF). He also held several director-ship appointments in public and private organisations, including the boards of Singapore Technologies Engineering, Defence Science and Technology Agency, and Jurong Town Corporation. Mr Ng graduated with a Bachelor of Science in Electrical Engineering from the United States Air Force Academy in 1991. In 2003, he obtained a Master of Arts (International Relations) from the Fletcher School of Law and Diplomacy at Tufts University.

ONG Ye Kung is currently Minister for Education (Higher Education and Skills) and Second Minister for Defence. He was appointed to the Cabinet of Singapore as Acting Minister for Education (Higher Education and Skills) and Senior Minister of State for Defence on 1 October 2015. Prior to his Cabinet appointment, he held senior positions at Keppel Corporation, and the National Trades Union Congress. He also held various positions in the government including the Singapore Workforce Development Agency where, as the Chief Executive, he spearheaded many initiatives to build up the Continuing Education and Training infrastructure. Mr Ong graduated from the London School of Economics and Political Science, United Kingdom, and holds a Master of Business Administration from the International Institute of Management Development, Lausanne, Switzerland.

Debra SOON is responsible for Profit and Loss, Programming, Marketing and Content Strategy for Singapore's free-to-air English entertainment television channel, *Channel 5*; radio stations *CLASS 95, GOLD 90.5, Exput Radio 96.3xfm, Symphony 924* and the magazine *8Days*. Ms Soon also manages TV operations across MediaCorp, including acquisitions, subtitling, content standards and broadcast playout. With over 20 years of experience in the media and communications industry, Ms Soon was appointed Managing Director of *Channel NewsAsia* in March 2009. She was responsible then for the editorial for English, Chinese, Malay and Tamil news and current affairs, as well as the business operations of *Channel NewsAsia*. Ms Soon is a Mentor and Member of BoardAgender and an Executive Committee Member of the Singapore Committee for UN Women, formerly known as UNIFEM Singapore. She is also on the Business Advisory Board of the Behavioural Sciences Institute of the Singapore Management University. Ms Soon obtained her BSc (Economics) and MSc (International Relations) from the London School of Economics and Political Science under scholarship from the Singapore Broadcasting Corporation, and later the Television Corporation of Singapore.

Eugene TAN is Associate Professor of Law at the Singapore Management University (SMU). He also co-directs the SMU Centre for Scholars' Development. Associate Professor Tan was educated at the National University of

Singapore, the London School of Economics and Political Science, and Stanford University where he was a Fulbright Fellow. He was admitted to the Singapore Bar in 1996. His inter-disciplinary research interests and teaching portfolio (in SMU's law, business, and social sciences schools) include law and public policy; constitutional and administrative law; the regulation of ethnic conflict; ethics and social responsibility; and the government and politics of Singapore. Between February 2012 and August 2014, Associate Professor Tan served as a Nominated Member of Parliament in Singapore's 12th Parliament.

TAN Kong Yam is presently Professor of Economics at the Nanyang Technological University and the Co-Director of the Asia Competitiveness Institute at the Lee Kuan Yew School of Public Policy, National University of Singapore. He was the Chief Assistant to Dr Goh Keng Swee (1985–1988), the former Deputy Prime Minister of Singapore invited by Mr Deng Xiaoping to advise China on economic development strategy. He was a Senior Economist at the World Bank office in Beijing (2002–2005). Prior to that, he was the Chief Economist of the Singapore government (1999–2002) and Head of Department of Strategy and Policy at the National University of Singapore Business School. He is a graduate of Princeton and Stanford University. His research interests are in international trade and finance, economic and business trends in the Asia Pacific region and economic reforms in China. He has published 10 books and numerous articles in major international journals. He served as Board Member at the Singapore Central Provident Fund Board (1984–1996), National Productivity Board (1989–1990), CapitaMalls Asia (2009–2014), and Changi Airport (since 2015). He has also consulted for many organisations including Temasek, GIC, Citigroup, IBM and China Construction Bank.

TENG Siao See is a Research Fellow at the Institute of Policy Studies. Trained as a sociologist, Dr Teng has taught and researched at varsities in the United Kingdom, Taiwan and Singapore. Her research interests include ethnic Chinese identities, inter-ethnic relations and diversity and equity in education. Dr Teng is currently undertaking research investigating parents' perception of education in Singapore and the role of parents in mediating students' academic stress. She has also conducted research on inter-ethnic harmony and migrant integration in Singapore.

YEOH Lam Keong is an Adjunct Professor at the Lee Kuan Yew School of Public Policy. He is a prominent economist in Singapore and is heavily involved in public policy research and commentary. He was formerly Chief Economist of the GIC for over 10 years. He has also been an Advisor or Fellow to a number of research institutes including the Institute of Policy Studies, the Civil Service College, Singapore Centre for Applied Policy Economics at the National University of Singapore. He also sits on the Singapore Management University School of Economics Advisory Board. He has worked on public policy with a number of key ministries, companies and major consulting firms.

www.ingramcontent.com/pod-product-compliance
Lightning Source LLC
Chambersburg PA
CBHW050607280326
41932CB00016B/2950